# JACOB
## DISCERNING GOD'S PRESENCE

# Also available in the Studies in Faithful Living Series

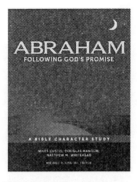

*Abraham: Following God's Promise*

*Joseph: Understanding God's Purpose*

*Mary: Devoted to God's Plan*

For updates on this series, visit LexhamPress.com/SFL

# JACOB
## DISCERNING GOD'S PRESENCE

Studies in Faithful Living

Derek R. Brown
Miles Custis
Douglas Mangum
Wendy Widder

**Editor**

John D. Barry

LEXHAM PRESS

*Jacob: Discerning God's Presence*
Studies in Faithful Living

Copyright 2014 Lexham Press

Lexham Press, 1313 Commercial St., Bellingham, WA 98225
LexhamPress.com

ISBN 978-1-57799580-7

Assistant Editors: Rebecca Brant, Lynnea Fraser, Elizabeth Vince
Cover Design: Jim LePage, Christine Gerhart
Typesetting: ProjectLuz.com

# TABLE OF CONTENTS

# INTRODUCTION

The struggles of Jacob's life start before his birth, and the biblical narrative of his life is colored by an intense back story of God's plan for humanity. He is born to an heir to a great promise from God, Isaac. Jacob's life is all about God's presence, but that doesn't mean he sees things that way.

Looking at the major events that make up the lives of people like Jacob is one way to engage with the story of the Bible. This is the approach taken by the Studies in Faithful Living series. In this volume, we examine the life of a twin brother who struggled against his own kin from the womb to old age, until eventually he learned what it meant to allow God's presence to define his life. Unlike the lives of some biblical characters, Jacob's journey is the antithesis of God's desires for us. In spite of Jacob grabbing at his brother's heel (and everything else), God continued to grab ahold of him. If Jacob had only responded in his early years, his life would have been filled with wonderment, beauty, and perhaps even positive life change for others. God doesn't want Jacob's earlier responses from us; he wants Jacob's later response—recognition that God's presence is with us always, everywhere. Nonetheless, the negative moments of Jacob's life are great lessons for him and for us. Studying the Bible in this way teaches us to model the exceptional characters of Scripture and to learn from their mistakes as well as their triumphs. Their lives can help us to grow in our efforts to imitate Christ. In doing so, we enter more deeply into the story the Bible narrates for us: God's redemption of creation—a story that continues in the lives of all those who respond to him today.

We begin in Chapter 1 by putting the story of Jacob in context. He received the blessing God gave to Abraham and passed on to his son, Isaac.

God promised that Abraham's descendants would be as numerous as the stars and that he would inherit what came to be known as the promised land. In Chapter 2, we find ourselves in the middle of what will become a ferocious struggle between the twin brothers, Esau and Jacob. This struggle has ramifications for God's people for years to come. Chapter 3 tells of Jacob's journey away from his family and his first direct encounter with God. Chapter 4 finds Jacob laboring as hired help and tricked into in a messy marital situation. Chapter 5 follows Jacob further into adversity as he attempts to free himself and his family from the controlling Laban. In Chapter 6, Jacob revisits his shattered past and pleads for God's protection as he encounters the person he had most injured during his earlier years of deception. Chapter 7 explores a dark period of Jacob's life when he neglects his family in a horrible situation with atrocious consequences. Chapter 8 brings us to Jacob's breakthrough moment—finally discerning God's presence, protection, and provision throughout his life in spite of Jacob's struggles against him. Throughout the study, we see Jacob's personal ambitions come head to head with God's desire to fill his life with his presence. We witness Jacob slowly learning to let God accomplish his will for his life.

To help you dig deeper into these biblical accounts, we've arranged each chapter into five sections. In *Setting the Stage*, we introduce the theme of the chapter and the significant literary, historical, and cultural details of the story at hand. *A Closer Look* illuminates the narrative by walking you through the story itself. *Throughout the Bible* connects the Old and New Testaments and shows how the biblical authors have understood the story under consideration at various points in biblical history. *Beyond the Bible* accomplishes a similar task by exploring the story within various historical contexts. This leads to the *Application*, where we discuss the relevance of Jacob's experiences for our lives today. Application and reflection questions conclude each chapter to help you contemplate and internalize what you've learned.

Ultimately, the underlying theme of Jacob's story connects directly with our experiences today. In Jacob's poor decision-making, rebellion, deceitfulness, and painful struggles, we see ourselves—either who we are, who we were, or who we could become. In the process, we learn that God does not give up on people, and that his purposes are not dependent on us discerning his presence or acting upon his will. However, when we do respond in obedience, we experience the richness of his presence on the journey. When we are what God meant for us to be—people who live as those who truly know him through Christ—we become something much greater than we could have ever been on our own. Our efforts to enhance our own image fade away, and God's presence in our lives becomes most valued. But aside from our steps and missteps, God will still go to extraordinary measures to accomplish his will and show his love to us (John 3:16–17). Jacob's life is a testament to that.

## CHAPTER 1

# PASSING ON THE PROMISE

*Read Genesis 24:1–67; 25:19–28.*

## SETTING THE STAGE

**Theme.** If someone asked you to tell the story of your life, where would you begin? Would you start with your childhood? Maybe you would look to events from before your birth, recounting your parents' meeting or your grandparents settling in a new country. Many of our life stories really begin with our ancestors. The same is true for biblical characters like Jacob, whose story is rooted in the lives of his father and grandfather and their relationship with God.

God had promised Abraham offspring as numerous as the stars. But from the very beginning of Jacob's story, Abraham's line was still in its humble beginnings. Dedicated to seeing God's covenantal promise passed on to future generations, Abraham sent his servant to the city of Nahor to seek out a wife for the child of promise, Isaac (Gen 24). When God providentially led the servant to Rebekah, we as readers are prepared for the birth of the next promise bearer. Instead, we learn that Rebekah was barren, like Sarah before her. God must intervene once again to continue the line of Abraham (Gen 25:21). In the prologue to Jacob's birth, we see that no circumstances or obstacles can prevent God from showing his loving faithfulness to his people.

**Literary Context.** With the son of promise, Isaac, grown into a man, Abraham looked to the next generation for the fulfillment of God's covenantal promises. He sent his servant to Mesopotamia with orders to find a wife for Isaac from his family (Gen 24:1–10). When the faithful servant stopped at a well to let his camels drink, he met Rebekah, the daughter of Abraham's brother (Gen 24:11–21). Upon receiving confirmation from God and permission from her family, the servant brought Rebekah back to Canaan, where she married Isaac (Gen 28:61–67).

Rebekah would shape her sons' lives in many ways. When she was still enduring her turbulent pregnancy, with her twin sons fighting in her womb, she received word from God that her younger son would prevail over her older son (Gen 25:23). After giving birth, she favored her younger son, Jacob, over her older son, Esau (Gen 25:28). Determined to see Jacob prevail, she devised a plan to trick her husband into blessing Jacob instead of Esau (Gen 27:5–17; see Chapter 2).

As this plan unfolds, Jacob flees to Mesopotamia, making the same journey Abraham's servant made (Gen 28:1–5). Many elements of Abraham's servant's venture reappear in Jacob's story, as if he is retracing the steps of the past. Just as Abraham's servant met Jacob's mother, Rebekah, at a well, Jacob will also meet his wife, Rachel, at a well (Gen 29:1–12). Laban, introduced here as Rebekah's brother, will play a large role in Jacob's life, as he will spend 14 years serving Laban for the right to marry his daughters (Gen 29:13–30; see Chapter 4).

Between the story of finding a wife for Isaac and the birth of his sons, Jacob and Esau, the biblical text focuses on Abraham's death and a brief summary of his life (Gen 25:1–18). This account concludes the Abraham narrative that began in Genesis 11:27.[1] It also gives the genealogy of Ishmael, Abraham's son through Hagar, and emphasizes that Isaac was the heir of God's promise to Abraham (Gen 25:11; compare Gen 17:18–21). With this reminder, we continue with the account of God's fulfillment of his promises to Abraham.

**Historical & Cultural Background.** As Abraham neared the end of his life (Gen 24:1), he began to focus on securing a wife for his son and heir, Isaac (Gen 21:12). It was standard practice in the ancient Near East for parents to arrange marriages for their children. It was also common for people to marry within their family or clan, a practice known as endogamy.

This practice preserved family inheritance and kept individual clans separate from outsiders or foreigners.[2] Wanting to preserve God's promise for his son and future generations, Abraham sought a wife for Isaac from among his own family. Later, we will see that Isaac's older son, Esau, went against this practice by marrying two Hittite women (Gen 26:34–35).

It was also customary in the ancient Near East for the husband's family to pay a "bride price" (*mohar*; see Exod 22:17) to the young woman's family. This monetary gift functioned as part of the negotiations for the arranged marriage, serving as a nuptial present. Once agreed upon, the bride price was considered a legal transaction. Ancient Near Eastern law codes included rules for what should be done with the bride price if an engagement was broken. For example, the *Code of Hammurabi* stated that if a man changed his mind about marrying a woman after giving the bride price, then her father could keep the bride price. On the other hand, if a father changed his mind and refused to give his daughter to a man who had already paid a bride price, then he was required to pay back twice the bride price.[3]

> **Quick Bit:** The *Code of Hammurabi* is an ancient Babylonian law code. It was enacted by Hammurabi, who reigned for 43 years around the 18th century BC. It consists of 282 laws covering a variety of matters such as property rights, marriage and divorce, compensation for injury, and theft. It shares many similarities with the Mosaic law.

Other valuable gifts (*mattān*; see Gen 34:12) could also be given to members of the bride's family, such as expensive jewelry and garments. In Genesis 24, Abraham's servant presented silver and gold jewelry to Rebekah and "costly ornaments" to Rebekah's brother (Laban) and mother (Gen 24:53). It is unclear whether these gifts functioned as a bride price or were simply gifts. While the term for bride price (*mohar*) is not used in the passage, the gifts may have served that function.

Regardless of these gifts' technical role, they demonstrated to Rebekah's family that Abraham was wealthy—an incentive for Rebekah's family to allow her to return with Abraham's servant and marry his son. Abraham's servant returned to Canaan with Rebekah, who was prepared to take on her role as the future mother of the promised heir, Jacob.

## A CLOSER LOOK

Although Isaac is regarded as one of Israel's patriarchs, he appears only as a minor character in the overall narrative of Genesis. Almost as soon as Abraham dies and Isaac receives God's blessing (Gen 25:7–11), the story focuses not on Isaac, but on his sons, Esau and Jacob. Still, Isaac serves as a crucial link between Abraham, to whom God first gave the promise, and Jacob, whom God would make into a great nation.

As Isaac reached marriageable age, Abraham recognized it was time to find him a wife from his family (Gen 24:4). Having seen God's blessing in preserving Isaac before (Gen 22:1–19), Abraham again demonstrates deep trust in God's promise to bless the world through his family.

To find a wife for Isaac, Abraham planned to send his eldest servant to his homeland, Aram-Naharaim. Before sending him on his way, however, Abraham made him swear an oath by "the LORD, the God of heaven and God of the earth" that he would only take a wife from his kindred and not from the Canaanites (Gen 24:3–4). The servant initially expressed his concern that a woman might not follow him back to the land of Canaan. But Abraham commanded that only the servant, not Isaac (Gen 24:6), should travel to his country and kindred and return with a wife for Isaac. Abraham's servant accepted this mission and swore an oath to his master.

> **Quick Bit:** Oaths in the ancient world were often made by taking hold of a significant object. Here, the servant places his hand under Abraham's thigh (Gen 24:9) to swear the oath. The intimate nature of this placement likely signifies the Abrahamic covenant—circumcision—which now depended on the servant's appointed task of finding a wife for Isaac, the heir of God's promise to Abraham. That the oath, made in the name of "the LORD, the God of heaven and God of the earth" (Gen 24:3 ESV) recalls Abraham's oath in Genesis 14:22.

Although Genesis 24 is ultimately about Abraham's desire to provide Isaac with a wife, the main character of the chapter is Abraham's servant. The Genesis narrative doesn't reveal the servant's name, nor does the servant give his name (but later tradition identifies the servant as Eliezer, mentioned in Gen 15:2). In Genesis 24, the servant introduces himself only in relation to the one who sent him: "Abraham's servant"

(Gen 24:34). His presence throughout the narrative of Genesis 24 indicates his importance to the preservation of God's promise to Abraham. If the servant were to fail and return without a wife for Isaac, God's plan to bless humanity through Abraham could be in jeopardy. But God will use this humble servant to accomplish his purpose—a motif that runs throughout Genesis and the rest of the Bible.

The servant departed for the city of Nahor in Aram-Naharaim, taking with him 10 of Abraham's camels and "all sorts of choice gifts from his master" (Gen 24:10 ESV)—luxurious gifts likely reserved for the future bride's family. Upon arriving in Nahor, the servant immediately began his search for Isaac's wife. His urgency seems to match that of his master (Gen 24:1-4). He knew he must find a wife for Isaac before Abraham died.

When he reached a well outside the city where women would come to draw water, the servant stopped to pray for God to grant him success in finding Isaac's wife. He asked God to show his "steadfast love" (*chesed*; Gen 24:12, 14, 27, 49) to Abraham by helping him find the right woman. The servant was specific in his request: He asked God to reveal as Isaac's wife the woman who would respond to his request for a drink from her jar and water for his camels (Gen 24: 13-14). Before the servant had even finished praying, God answered his prayer—a young woman named Rebekah approached with a water jar on her shoulder and offered water to him and his camels.

With God's confirmation that Rebekah was the chosen wife for Isaac, the servant lavished her with gifts of jewelry and asked about her father and household. When Rebekah divulges her family's identity and invites the servant to stay with them, he breaks into praise:

> "Blessed be the LORD, the God of my master Abraham, who has not forsaken his steadfast love (*chesed*) and his faithfulness toward my master. As for me, the LORD has led me in the way to the house of my master's kinsmen" (Gen 24:27 ESV).

Rebekah traveled ahead of the servant to tell "her mother's household" of her encounter with the man. When Rebekah's brother, Laban—introduced here and later to play a key role in Jacob's life—spotted the costly gifts given to Rebekah and recognized that God's favor was with

Abraham's servant, he immediately went out to the man and invited him into their household.

Accepting their hospitality, the servant delivered a long speech recounting everything that has happened so far in the narrative (Gen 24:34–49). The speech might seem redundant to us, since it repeats what we've already read, but it provided essential information for Rebekah's family. The servant specifically mentioned Abraham's wealth (Gen 24:35), a detail that would have interested them. He concluded his speech with two important features: He offered praise to "the God of my master Abraham" (Gen 24:48), then asked for Rebekah to become the wife of his master's son (Gen 24:49).

Laban and Bethuel, Rebekah's mother, immediately agreed to give Rebekah as Isaac's wife, recognizing God's hand in the events: "This is clearly from the LORD, and we cannot change what must happen" (Gen 24:50). In response, the servant again worshiped God for his provision (Gen 24:52). He then distributed the gifts he brought from Abraham (Gen 24:10): fine jewelry and garments for Rebekah and "expensive gifts" for her brother and mother (Gen 24:53).

The next morning, the servant departed with Rebekah for the land of Canaan (Gen 24:59). As they left, Rebekah's family blessed her, wishing her abundant offspring (Gen 24:60). The passage that began in blessing for Abraham (Gen 24:1) now ends in great blessing for Rebekah, the future mother of the promised heir.

The servant and Rebekah returned from Abraham's land to find Isaac awaiting them in the Negev. After their initial introduction, Isaac and Rebekah married, fulfilling Abraham's efforts to secure the future of God's promise.

The entire story of Genesis 24 is told within the context of God's providential care for Abraham and his descendants. From beginning to end, Abraham's plan to find his son a wife unfolds with little difficulty. The servant, like his master, demonstrated great trust in God through worship and prayer (Gen 24:12–14, 26–27, 52). Even Laban and Bethuel acknowledged that Abraham's servant had been sent by God (Gen 24:50). Everyone in the story acted "as the LORD has spoken" (24:51 ESV) to ensure that God's will would be accomplished without hurdle or delay.

Yet as the narrative continues, a situation arises with the potential to threaten the fulfillment of God's covenantal blessing: Rebekah, like Sarah (and later, Rachel), was barren. Isaac and Rebekah spent 20 years in uncertainty over whether they would have a son who would continue the covenantal promise—20 years that the narrative collapses into a few short verses (Gen 25:20, 26). Isaac prayed for God to intervene and trusted him for the outcome. The narrative gives no clue as to how much time passed after Isaac's prayer, but God eventually answered, allowing Rebekah to become pregnant (Gen 25:21)—and not with just one baby, but with two.

Rebekah's pregnancy did not go smoothly. As the "children in her womb jostled each other," she cried to God for an explanation: "If it is going to be like this, why be pregnant?" (Gen 25:22). God answered with a prophetic pronouncement that foretold future strife between her two sons. God's pronouncement also contains a detail that plays a significant role in Jacob's story: "And the elder shall serve the younger."

We can't be sure what Rebekah made of the bewildering pronouncement. Perhaps it dictated her own behavior as she tried to steer her favored son toward superiority over his older brother. Perhaps she told Jacob of God's words, and he joined her efforts to secure his own fortune. It's not clear exactly what God's words to Rebekah indicate: like many oracles, the phrasing appears deliberately ambiguous.[4] Is this a pronouncement of what *will* happen or a prediction of what *might* happen *if other actions are not taken*? In other words, is this a warning or a prophecy? Whatever the case, the narrative never directly refers to this oracle again. Instead, it's used to set the stage for the rest of Jacob's story.

When Rebekah gave birth to her tussling infants—first to Esau, then to Jacob, who "came out with his hand grasping Esau's heel" (Gen 25:26 NIV)—we already recognize which roles each son will play in God's plan for covenantal blessing, but the tension is still present. The quiet, tent-dwelling younger brother will struggle to gain superiority over his rugged, hairy brother (Gen 25:25–28). Almost as soon as the story begins, Jacob does so when he buys Esau's birthright with a pot of stew. But just after being blessed with the birthright, he has to run from his angry brother. It will be more than 20 years before the brothers meet again, and, ironically, Jacob will bow before "[his] lord, Esau" (Gen 32:4) Only then will the patriarch return to the promised land to take possession of his inheritance.

In the end, what God proclaimed to Rebekah proves true, and Jacob comes to recognize his role in carrying on the promise God made to Abraham.

## THROUGHOUT THE BIBLE

The brief prophetic story of the birth of Jacob and Esau in Genesis 25:19–28 carries considerable significance in the Bible. It not only anticipates the remainder of the Jacob story (Gen 25:27–34; 27:1–28:9; 32:3–33:17), but it also becomes a paradigm for the relationship between Israel and Edom—the two nations for which Jacob and Esau serve, respectively, as eponymous heads. True to God's word to Rebekah in Genesis 25:23, the story of Israel and Edom reflects that of Jacob and Esau in Genesis: a violent struggle between rival brothers.

Numbers 20 tells of the Israelites' request for permission from the "king of Edom" (Num 20:14–21) to pass through the land of Edom. The king refuses and threatens the Israelites, forcing the nation to travel around Edom to reach Canaan. In the historical books, we learn of Saul's campaigns and David's large-scale military success against the Edomites (1 Sam 14:47; 2 Sam 8:14). In the later period of the kings, Edom revolted against Judah (2 Kings 8:22), but was unable to regain its independence at the time.

In their oracles of judgment against Edom, the prophets in particular drew upon the Jacob and Esau contrast. Both Isaiah and Jeremiah issue judgment oracles against Edom (Isa 34:5–17; Jer 49:7–22), but the tradition is epitomized in the short prophetic book of Obadiah, which focuses almost exclusively on the failures of Edom and God's disgust with them. Writing directly against the nation of Edom, Obadiah chastises Judah's neighbor for its behavior during the destruction of Jerusalem (587 BC). Obadiah recasts the story of Jacob and Esau as a metaphor for the struggle of Judah (and Israel) against Edom.

At the heart of Obadiah's oracle against Edom is the nation's complicit behavior during Judah's time of need. Although the Edomites were relatives of the Israelites, they allowed foreigners to attack and pillage Jerusalem (Obad 11). Even worse, Edom gloated over Judah's misfortune and joined in the looting of the city (Obad 12–13; see also Ezek 25:12–14;

35:1–15). God condemned Edom for treating its brother, Judah, as an enemy and—as Genesis 25:23 foresaw—Obadiah predicts the triumph of the house of Jacob, the younger brother, over the house of Esau, the older brother. In the end, the house of Esau will be utterly destroyed, and the remnant of Jacob will "go up on Mount Zion to rule the mountain of Esau" (Obad 21).

The motif of enmity between Jacob and Esau in the OT demonstrates how the biblical authors believed the story of the twin brothers was significant for the ongoing history of God's people. Even when Edom seemed to have the upper hand over its younger brother, Israel (sometimes represented as Judah) held out hope (e.g., Obad 15–21) that, with God's aid, they would eventually prevail over their older sibling just as Jacob prevailed over Esau in Genesis.

## BEYOND THE BIBLE

God is always at work in the world, even when obstacles seem to threaten his promised future. God promised Abraham that he would make him a great nation (Gen 12:2). After years of waiting, this promise saw its initial fulfillment in the birth of Isaac. When Isaac's wife was barren, God demonstrated that no obstacle can hinder his plans. Later, God blessed Isaac and Rebekah with two sons, albeit ones who shared a tenuous relationship even within the womb.

> **Quick Bit:** The book of *Jubilees* presents itself as a direct account of God's revelation to Moses on Sinai. The "angel of the presence" provides Moses with a firsthand narrative explaining everything "from the first creation until [God's] sanctuary is built in their midst" (Jubilees 1:27).[5] This covers the material from Genesis 1 to Exodus 20 and organizes the account according to "jubilees" or 49-year time spans representing seven periods of seven years each. The text was written in Hebrew, probably in the mid-second century BC. *Jubilees* primarily repeats and expands stories from the biblical books of Genesis and Exodus.

God did not formally pass the promise to Jacob until Genesis 28:13–15, but the biblical account hints that, just like the events with Isaac and

Ishmael, the normal inheritance of the firstborn will fall to the second son (Gen 25:23). The subtle ways that later writers addressed this issue reflects their concern to legitimize Jacob's chosen status from the beginning. The book of *Jubilees* expands on the stories of Genesis, and takes a special interest in explaining how Jacob, the second son, came to be the son through whom the promises to Abraham were continued:

> And in the sixth week in the second year Rebecca bore two children for Isaac, Jacob and Esau. And Jacob was smooth and upright, but Esau was a fierce man and rustic and hairy. And Jacob used to dwell in the tents. And the youths grew up and Jacob learned writing, but Esau did not learn because he was a rustic man and a hunter. And he learned war, and all of his deeds were fierce. And Abraham loved Jacob, but Isaac loved Esau. And Abraham saw the deeds of Esau and he knew that in Jacob a name and seed would be named for him (*Jubilees* 19:13–16).[6]

The biblical writer sets up the sibling rivalry by playing one parent against the other: Isaac loved Esau, but Rebekah loved Jacob (Gen 25:28). *Jubilees* takes this one step further. It is not enough that Jacob was the favorite son of the matriarch; he must also have the stamp of approval from a patriarch. To achieve that end, the writer of *Jubilees* claims that Jacob was also Abraham's favorite, and somehow Abraham knew that Jacob was the chosen son.

In retelling Jacob's story, *Jubilees* follows a common pattern from ancient Jewish and Christian writings about the Bible, in which foreshadowing becomes explicit. In the biblical narrative, Jacob was chosen by God but took his place as the child of promise through a series of deceptions. In *Jubilees*, Jacob deserved his position by merit of his cultured nature and education, factors noted by his grandfather. This pattern is common even today when we read the Bible or watch world events. We feel there must be a rational reason behind God's selection of one person and not another. We attempt to interpret events in our own lives to find the reason why God led us one way and not another. This human tendency is hard to break, but we need to remember that only God knows the big and entire picture and trust him for the outcome.

## APPLICATION

We often think of God as working in extremes. We expect him to accomplish great things through the lives of exceptional people and to work through miracles and awesome displays of power. Rarely do we see his hand in the ordinary and everyday. In the events leading up to Jacob's birth, we find an antidote to both of these misguided perceptions. In Genesis 24–25, God accomplishes his purposes through an ordinary servant and a miracle of healing. In both cases, he acted in response to the prayers of the humble and faithful (Gen 24:12–15; 25:21).

In Abraham's servant, we find a model for how to approach God in humility and trust. At all major points of the story, the servant prays for God's blessing and worships God when he answers. In Isaac, we find belief in God's power to heal. When Rebekah's barrenness becomes evident, Isaac "prayed to Yahweh on behalf of his wife" (Gen 25:21). God answered Isaac's prayer, blessing him and Rebekah with children—one who would become heir to the covenantal promise.

The Bible provides us with many examples of faithful prayer—from Solomon to Daniel (1 Kgs 8:45; Dan 6:10). And like these biblical characters, we may encounter obstacles and setbacks on our journeys of faith. We may find ourselves on missions that seem hopeless or in seasons of barrenness and despair. But like Abraham's servant and Isaac, we can be confident that God is eager to meet us in our times of need, if only we appeal to him. The author of Hebrews writes, "Therefore let us approach with confidence to the throne of grace, in order that we may receive mercy and find grace to help in time of need" (Heb 4:16). Like these two role models, we can turn to prayer and worship to sustain us along our journeys of faith. When we approach God earnestly and humbly through prayer, we can be confident that he will answer.

# DISCUSSION

**A Closer Look**

1. In what ways does this story show God's will being accomplished? How have you seen God's will being accomplished in your life?

_____

_____

_____

2. How do Abraham's servant and Isaac demonstrate their trust in God? Do you rely on God in the same way?

_____

_____

_____

**Throughout the Bible**

1. God prophesied that Esau would serve Jacob. How did Esau's decisions contribute to the fulfillment of this prophecy? How did Jacob's actions contribute to it?

_____

_____

_____

2. The relationship between Esau and Jacob set the stage for a struggle between two nations that would continue for centuries. Do you have any conflict with someone that has continued for a long time? What can you do to reconcile that situation?

_____

_____

_____

## Beyond the Bible

1. Reflect on a time when you tried to rationalize something inexplicable. What dangers do you see in doing so?

_____

_____

_____

2. Consider a time when what you thought was an obstacle actually directed you exactly where God wanted you to be.

_____

_____

_____

## Application

1. Do you seek God's hand only in the extremes? How can the stories of the Bible help you recognize God's hand in ordinary events?

_____

_____

_____

2. Abraham's servant showed remarkable perseverance throughout Genesis 24. What keeps you going in your service to God? What sets you back or discourages you the most?

_____

_____

_____

## CHAPTER 2

# BIRTHRIGHT AND BLESSING

*Read Genesis 25:29–34; 27:1–40.*

## SETTING THE STAGE

**Theme**. It only takes a few unwise actions to establish bad habits in our lives. We do something once or twice, and it becomes a normal part of our behavior. Often without us realizing it, these actions can embed themselves into our character and reputation. It's far more difficult to break a habit than build one—a lesson that Jacob learned the hard way.

Jacob entered the world clinging to the heel of his older twin brother, Esau (Gen 25:26), and he seems to spend the remainder of their adolescence nipping at Esau's heel in an attempt to overtake him. Eventually, through two acts of deceit, Jacob succeeded in depriving Esau of his rightful privileges as the firstborn. Jacob first took advantage of his brother's hunger, persuading him to exchange his birthright for food (Gen 25:29–34). Then Jacob deceived his father, Isaac, and robbed Esau of his blessing (Gen 27:1–40). Twice he benefited from deceit. For Jacob, deception developed into a character flaw he would wrestle with most of his life. Only a painful encounter with God himself (Gen 32:22–32) made Jacob begin to recognize the error of his ways.

**Literary Context.** The sibling rivalry that began while Jacob and Esau were still in Rebekah's womb only intensified as the boys grew up. It doesn't take long for the Genesis account of Jacob's story to become characterized by deceit. When Esau, exhausted and starved, approached

Jacob and pleaded for a bowl of his favorite stew, Jacob took advantage of his brother's weakness to bargain for his birthright (Gen 25:29-34). Then, when it came time for Esau to receive their father's blessing, Jacob again turned to deception, tricking Isaac into blessing him instead (Gen 27:1-40).

These incidents directly connect to the preceding account of Jacob and Esau's birth (Gen 25:19-28). Just as God foretold to the pregnant Rebekah (Gen 25:23), Jacob prevailed over his older brother, gaining Esau's birthright and blessing. Isaac and Rebekah's differing favoritism of their twin sons, first mentioned in Genesis 25:27-28, only fueled the boys' antagonism and led to Jacob's triumph. To make matters worse, it was Rebekah who suggested that Jacob, her favorite son, should trick Isaac into blessing him instead of Esau.

Elements of these two events foreshadow and characterize much of Jacob's later story. His life is defined by his relationship with his rival sibling; it begins with his conflict with Esau (Gen 25:19-34; 27:1-45; 27:46-28:9) and ends with their reconciliation (Gen 32-33:17). Jacob's strained relationships with Esau and Isaac prefigure his later struggles with his family (Gen 31:22-42). And Jacob's lifelong tendency to ensure his prosperity at the expense of others originates in these two accounts of his deception of Esau.

**Historical & Cultural Background.** In the ancient world, the firstborn son held a unique position among his siblings. According to the cultural custom of primogeniture, the family name and title was passed on through the eldest son. The firstborn also received a double portion of the inheritance (Deut 21:17). In addition, birth order also determined the distribution of further family rights and inheritance.

The second son by mere moments, Jacob prized his older brother's birthright and eventually succeeded in gaining it for himself. Esau's seemingly indifferent attitude toward his birthright—trading it for a bowl of stew after a long day of hunting—brought shame upon him in the biblical tradition. Genesis 25:34 condemns Esau's careless decision, commenting that he "despised his birthright." The book of Hebrews shares this well-established characterization, warning its readers not to be unholy like Esau, "who for one meal traded his own birthright" and failed to regain his father's blessing "because he did not find an occasion for repentance, although he sought it with tears" (Heb 12:16–17). Yet Esau's carelessness doesn't justify Jacob's treachery.

Perhaps, as one scholar suggests, Jacob already knew about God's promise to Rebekah—made while he was still in the womb—and thus acted to gain what he believed was rightfully his.[1] Whatever the case, Jacob's ambitious ploys to obtain Esau's birthright and blessing (Gen 27:1–40) resulted in a reversal of fortune that was anticipated in the divine promise to Rebekah. As Jacob's story unfolds, we continue to find exceptions to the cultural norms of blessing and inheritance. Jacob will strip his firstborn, Reuben, of his expected portion of the inheritance because of his acts of incest (Gen 49:3–4; 35:22–23). When it came time for the elderly Jacob to give his own blessing, he gave it to Joseph's sons instead of his own (Gen 48:1–22; compare 1 Chr 5:1–2), blessing Ephraim, the younger son, over the older Manasseh (Gen 48:13–20).

## A CLOSER LOOK

The two accounts in Genesis 25:29–34 and Genesis 27:1–40 give us a first glimpse at Jacob's adult life. They tell similar stories marked by deceit and trickery as Jacob schemed to gain what rightfully belonged to his older brother, Esau. By successfully obtaining Esau's birthright and blessing, Jacob altered the lineage of the patriarchal family—he assumed the role of heir, and Esau was demoted to the status of the younger brother. These accounts reveal Jacob's true character as a schemer who was willing to use others—at their expense—to get ahead or protect himself.

In the first of these two stories, Jacob seized a seemingly unexpected opportunity for his own gain. Esau, the skilled hunter, returned from the field exhausted and noticed the "red stew" that Jacob, the peaceful man who lived in tents (Gen 25:27), had prepared. Exhausted from his hunt, Esau asked his younger brother for some stew. Jacob responded shrewdly, demanding his brother's birthright in exchange for the food. Jacob knew he had the upper hand over his weakened, weary brother. Esau gave in, acknowledging that his birthright would be of no value to him if he died. The story ends with a rare value judgment in Genesis: "Esau despised his birthright" (Gen 25:34).

**Quick Bit:** Esau referred to Jacob's food as "red stuff" (*adom*), re-calling a similar sounding Hebrew word used in Genesis 25:25 to describe Esau's reddish color (*admowni*). According to the Genesis narrative, Esau's desire for "red stuff" explains the name later given to him and his descendants: Edom (*edom*). Collectively, the Hebrew wordplay illustrates the fulfillment of the Genesis 25:23 oracle's pre-diction concerning two nations.

Although Jacob now possessed his brother's birthright (*bekhorah*), he had not yet fully taken the place of the elder brother. To complete the subver-sion, Jacob also needed his father's blessing (*berakhah*), which is the focus of the second, longer story.

Just as Abraham's old age served as the backstory to Genesis 24, the story of Jacob's deception of Isaac occurred near the end of Isaac's life, when he "was old and his eyesight was weak" (Gen 27:1). By highlighting Isaac's old age, the narrative sets us up to expect that the God's promise to Abraham is about to be passed to the patriarch's firstborn son. Ironically, as the account unfolds, what should be the story about Isaac and Esau—a father and his rightful heir by birth—becomes the story of Rebekah and Jacob, a mother and her younger son.

Nearly blind, Isaac summoned his favored and firstborn son to his side. It was more common for a father to gather all his children to pronounce his blessing,[2] but Isaac's isolation of Esau unwittingly created an ideal op-portunity for Jacob. Isaac asked Esau, an excellent hunter (Gen 25:27), to bring him game from the field in preparation for the blessing he planned to bestow upon him. Esau obeyed, quickly heading out to hunt.

We are not told whether Isaac knew that others had heard his instruc-tions to Esau, but Rebekah's eavesdropping (Gen 27:5) paved the way for the following events. Recognizing an opportunity to assert her will upon the destiny of her favorite son (Gen 25:28), Rebekah proposed a plan to Jacob. Knowing that Esau's task of finding wild game would take time, she instructed Jacob to fetch goats from the family's flock. With this meat, she would prepare a delicious meal for Jacob to serve to Isaac in Esau's place (Gen 27:8–10).

Jacob's next step truly reveals his character. Rather than reacting with revulsion to the idea of deceiving his father, he pointed out a potential weak point in the plan: He had smooth skin, but his brother was hairy. If Isaac were to catch on to the ruse, would he curse Jacob instead of bless him (Gen 27:12)? Rebekah soothed Jacob's apprehensions, declaring that she was willing to take any curse upon herself for him to receive his father's blessing. But Rebekah also recognized that Jacob had a good point, so she ordered him to use the skins of the goats to disguise his smooth skin (Gen 25:16).

Bearing a plate of tasty food and adorned in Esau's clothes and goat skin, Jacob masqueraded as his brother. In a tension-filled scene, Jacob attempted to beguile his own father. When Jacob first appeared before his father, Isaac inquired about his visitor's identity: "Who are you, my son?" (Gen 27:18). Jacob seemed to recognize Isaac's suspicion and overreacted[3] in confirming his identity: "I am Esau, your firstborn. I have done as you told me. Please get up, sit up and eat from my wild game so that you may bless me" (Gen 27:19). Still doubtful, Isaac pressed further and commented on "Esau's" remarkable success in finding game. Jacob attributed his achievement to God, but Isaac wasn't convinced. Was this really the son he loved? To further test this "Esau," Isaac asked him to draw near so he could touch his hairy skin. Even though it appears he had recognized the voice of Jacob, Isaac was finally convinced of "Esau's" identity by his touch and smell (Gen 27:23, 27). He blessed the disguised Jacob and ate the food brought to him.

Jacob's act of duplicity not only worked, but it resulted in rich blessing for him. His father promised him agricultural abundance—"May God give you of the dew of heaven and of the fatness of the earth" (Gen 27:28)—as well as political dominance—"Let peoples serve you, and nations bow down to you" (Gen 27:29). Having obtained his father's blessing (*berakhah*), Jacob had now fully supplanted his older brother.

> **Quick Bit:** Pay attention to frequently repeated words and their cognates, which are often mirrored in English translations. In Genesis 27, the Hebrew root *b-r-k*, rendered "bless" or "blessing" in English, occurs 17 times as a verb and six times as a noun. By taking note of what words the biblical authors repeat, you can better understand the central themes and concepts of a particular passage. With Logos Bible Software, you can easily search—in English or an original language—for all the occurrences of a word or its root.

The significance of the preceding narrative becomes immediately evident when Esau returned from his hunt. Eager to please his father but unaware of Jacob's trickery, Esau entered in much the same fashion as his brother. Like Jacob, Esau offered his meal to Isaac in anticipation of receiving his father's blessing. Isaac seemed to immediately recognize that he had been tricked: "Who then was he that hunted wild game and brought it to me, and I ate it all before you came, and I blessed him? Moreover, he will be blessed!" (Gen 27:33). Although Isaac had taken care to verify the identity of his earlier visitor, he seemed to know the answer to his own question, as the later verses will tell us.

Isaac's response is one of fear and defeat; Esau's is one of outrage and desperation. Having learned that his father blessed someone else, he pathetically cried out, "Bless me as well, my father!" (Gen 27:34). Isaac then revealed to Esau what the reader already knows: "Your brother came in deceit and took your blessing" (Gen 27:35).

Esau's reply contains a play on similar Hebrew words. Previously, we learned that Esau's younger brother was given the name Jacob (*ya'aqov*), which means "to protect" (Gen 25:26). Here Esau rhetorically asks whether his brother is rightly named Jacob since he had twice "deceived" (*'aqab*) Esau. If Esau hadn't caught on after the first time Jacob tricked him, he was now convinced of his brother's character.

Although Esau acknowledged that Jacob had again deceived him, he was unwilling to accept reality. After asking whether Isaac reserved any blessing for his oldest son (Gen 27:36), Esau learned his fate within the family: He not only lost his rights and blessing as firstborn, but he would now be subject to his younger brother (Gen 27:37). Bursting into tears, Esau again begged his father for a blessing. Isaac finally complied, but his blessing for Esau is really an "antiblessing."[4] Esau would live, but he would also serve his brother and remain restless until he was no longer under Jacob's yoke.

Jacob's actions shouldn't surprise us. He had already conned his own brother into giving up his birthright, so his willingness to go along with his mother's plan for gaining Esau's blessing wasn't out of character. Having learned that he could leverage situations for his own favor, Jacob was prepared to take advantage of whomever he needed—including his family—if it could help him prosper. And although Jacob's deception marked the second time he fooled his brother, it would not be the last time he took advantage of a family member.

## THROUGHOUT THE BIBLE

While moments of Jacob's deception of Isaac may have left us holding our breath, his success in supplanting Esau had been foretold. God had told Rebekah that her younger son would prevail. God's choice of Jacob over Esau in Genesis 25 became a key passage about divine selection for later biblical writers as they attempted to explain the mystery of God's election. The Apostle Paul's use of the Jacob and Esau motif in his lengthy letter to the Romans is the most developed in the Bible.

In Romans 9, Paul addresses several questions concerning God's election raised by his explication of the gospel in Romans 1–8. At the core is the question of Israel's role in the new steps God was taking among the Gentiles, that is, non-Jews. Did the Gentiles' inclusion mean that God had rejected Israel and therefore abandoned his election of the nation as his chosen people? And if the Jewish people—whom God called to be a blessing to the world—had rejected God's plan to rescue all people through Jesus, then did God's own proclamations fail (Rom 9:6)?

Paul's response to these questions draws upon God's election of a chosen people in the ᴏᴛ, including the oracle about Jacob and Esau in Genesis 25:23. Paul argues that no one should be surprised by the inclusion of the Gentiles into God's people, since the basis of God's election (to the task of carrying out God's promise to Abraham) was never purely according to lineage (Rom 9:6–7). Not all of Abraham's direct descendants were true descendants; only those born of the heir of the promise—Isaac, and not Ishmael—were truly descendants of Abraham (Rom 9:7–9).

Paul then appeals to the oracle concerning Jacob and Esau in Genesis 25:23. Having established that God's call is not based on lineage, Paul now argues that it is also not confined to cultural customs. If God were limited to human standards, the promise would have been passed on through Esau, not his younger brother. But, Paul points out, Scripture tells us that God chose Jacob over Esau—the younger brother instead of the elder—*before* they were born (Rom 9:10-11), subverting the widespread cultural norms that gave preference to the eldest son. To illustrate this decision, Paul quotes God's words through the prophet Malachi: "Jacob I loved, but Esau I hated" (Rom 9:13; see Mal 1:2-3). Thus Paul can clarify his case that "it is not the children of the flesh [blood line relatives of Abraham] who are the children of God, but the children of the promise [who] are counted as descendants" (Rom 9:8 NRSV).

Having ruled out both lineage and cultural customs as the basis for God's call, Paul finally identifies the true foundation of divine election: God's mercy. Since all are sinners (Rom 3:22-23) and mere pieces of clay (Rom 9:21), no one—whether Esau or Pharaoh (Rom 9:17-18)—can object to God's election. The hope of salvation resides not in God's justice— since all are guilty—but in God's merciful goodness toward humanity. God's election is therefore his own prerogative, as Paul's quotation of Exodus 33:19 makes clear: "I will have mercy on whomever I have mercy, and I will have compassion on whomever I have compassion" (Rom 9:15).

Paul's conclusion is that Israel used to play the part of Jacob, the heir of promise, but now they play the role of Esau, the rightful heir who does not have the promise. God's promises now extend to the Gentiles as well. Those who receive God's promises, then, become his children. God's word has not failed (Rom 9:6).[5] Rather, his will has been fulfilled by the addition of the Gentiles, whose inclusion the prophets predicted (Rom 9:25-29).

God's sovereignty is inscrutable; his ways are a mystery to us. God's election—of Abraham, Jacob, Israel, and of Christians today—rests entirely in his mercy. As believers, our reflection on God's election should lead where it does for Paul—to praise of God's mercy:

> "Oh, the depth of the riches and the wisdom and the knowledge of God! How unsearchable are his judgments and how incomprehensible are his ways! 'For who has known the mind of the Lord, or who has been his counselor? Or who has given in advance to him, and it will be paid back to him?' For from him and through him and to him are all things. To him be glory for eternity! Amen" (Rom 11:33-36).

# BEYOND THE BIBLE

Jacob's actions reveal a pattern of selfish ambition and deceit—a far cry from the virtuous character we expect from a patriarch. Ancient interpreters of Genesis were often troubled by Jacob's questionable behavior. Genesis 27 exposes a man driven by personal gain, which led ancient readers to attempt to rescue Jacob from his legacy of deceitful behavior. The goal of these interpreters was to present Jacob as a model of virtue, which they accomplished by overlooking his faults to emphasize his faith. The book of *Jubilees* (Jub 26:13–19) and a rabbinic midrash both reread Genesis 27:18–19 in a way that absolves Jacob from the charge of lying to his father.

> **Quick Bit:** "Midrash" refers both to a method of rabbinic interpretation and to texts that use that method to offer commentary on the biblical text. These Jewish texts were written primarily in the middle and late centuries of the first millennium AD.

When Jacob approaches his father disguised as Esau, Isaac asks if the man entering his tent is one of his sons. Jacob replies, "I am Esau, your firstborn" (Gen 27:19). His answer seems pretty straightforward, but the midrash divides the words to produce a different meaning.

> And Jacob said, "I am Esau your firstborn." [The interpretation:] He stopped in the middle; he said, "I am" but "Esau is your firstborn."⁶

So Jacob wasn't lying after all. We've been misreading what he said this whole time. How is that possible? It's not, really. The midrash's solution isn't the most logical reading of the phrase, but it is grammatically possible. The Hebrew text of the Bible was written without vowels, punctuation, or any other marks that would explicitly indicate when one sentence ended and another began. These ancient interpreters took advantage of that flexibility. The Hebrew tendency to use clauses without verbs (where the verb "to be" is implied) for these short exchanges further aided their cause. The Hebrew phrase was only three words: *anokhiy esau bekhorekha* (very literally, "I Esau firstborn-your"). By dividing one sentence into two, they changed Jacob's answer. He told the truth.

He acknowledged that he was Isaac's son but clarified that Esau was really the firstborn.

However, this explanation doesn't really absolve Jacob of responsibility for his actions. He still covered his arms with skins so they would feel hairy like Esau's. He still offered Isaac food, passing it off as "game" and implying he'd had a quick and successful hunt (Gen 27:19-20). Later, when Isaac asked him point-blank, "Are you really Esau?" Jacob simply replied, "I am" (Gen 27:24).

Other ancient interpreters took a different approach in explaining Jacob's behavior. They admitted that Jacob was trying to trick his father but argued that God must have wanted Jacob to receive the blessing because Jacob's ruse wasn't all that clever.[7] This explanation, like most attempts to justify Jacob's deceptive actions, is feeble at best.

But we don't have to justify or agree with Jacob's actions to learn from his story. Through Jacob's life, we see that God loves everyone and can work through anyone—even people who struggle to behave morally. All people are susceptible to mistakes, missteps, and poor judgment. Although Jacob often acted in ways that were contrary to God's character, God had a plan for him. He would work in Jacob's life despite his flaws.

## APPLICATION

Bad habits and character flaws are difficult to change. Many of us go through our entire lives ensnared by sinful impulses and corrosive patterns of thought. As believers, we may recognize the need for change and attempt to correct our hearts and behavior. Yet, in reality, our fallen nature—what Paul calls our "flesh" (Greek *sarx*)—constantly drives us to act for our own gain—our autonomy, our pleasure, our pride. As Christians, we take part in a perpetual battle between the desire of our flesh and the Spirit (Gal 5:16-17).

After benefiting from deceit, Jacob goes on to fight a losing battle against the flesh. Tricking his brother Esau into selling him his birthright (Gen 25:29-34) and his father into endowing him with the blessing of the firstborn (Gen 27:1-29) was only the beginning. Later, Jacob prospered at the expense of his uncle, Laban (Gen 30:25-43). It seems as though once Jacob began deceiving others, he couldn't stop. Jacob's self-serving actions also show a lack of faith. In the end, it took a painful encounter with God (Gen 32:22-32) for Jacob to realize God's presence in his life and to change how he treated others (see Gen 33:1-11). Yet through all the lies, the deception, and the deceit, God's continued to pursue Jacob.

Jacob's story and Paul's struggle against the "flesh" do not leave us hopeless, or excuse poor decisions, for Paul also states that in Christ we are a "new creation." We are raised to a new life through and because of Christ—a life in which sin has been conquered, and we are empowered to live free of it (2 Cor 5:16-17; Rom 6:1-14).

# DISCUSSION

## A Closer Look

1. Jacob and Rebekah used deception to obtain Isaac's blessing. Were they wrong to do so? Is there a situation where using deception is acceptable? Why or why not?

_____

_____

_____

2. Jacob's deception and manipulation of Esau sets a pattern of behavior for him. Are there any negative patterns of behavior in your life? How can you break out of them?

_____

_____

_____

## Throughout the Bible

1. How does Paul's argument in Romans 9 help you understand God's election?

_____

_____

_____

2. It is easy as a Christian to take God's mercy for granted. What are some practical ways you can recall the mercy God has shown you in your life?

_____

_____

_____

**Beyond the Bible**

1. Are you plagued by feelings of inferiority and failure? How can confidence in God's love for you and his plan for your life help you overcome those feelings?

_____

_____

_____

2. Think about a time when you tried to retell a story to emphasize the positive. Did you feel like you were being dishonest? Would the truth have conveyed a more powerful point?

_____

_____

_____

**Application**

1. What habits or flaws are entrenched in your character? How did these habits begin for you?

_____

_____

_____

2. What would it take for you to begin to change this habit or flaw?

_____

_____

_____

## CHAPTER 3

# DREAMING OF THE DIVINE

*Read Genesis 27:41–28:22.*

## SETTING THE STAGE

**Theme.** Loneliness is a common side effect of suffering. When we're enduring hardship, we can feel completely isolated from others. It can even become difficult to discern God's presence in our lives. Discouraged, isolated, and perhaps despairing, we are tempted to think God has abandoned us. But he is always there, even when distress and loneliness overwhelm us.

After he succeeded in defrauding his father to gain Esau's blessing, Jacob may have expected his life to improve. But his stolen success came at a cost. Infuriated, Esau was determined to kill Jacob as soon as their father died. So, with the excuse of seeking a wife among his mother's relatives, Jacob fled for his life. Alone and fearful, Jacob must have felt that God had abandoned him. But God reached through Jacob's despair, vividly appearing to him and extending the promise to Jacob that he had made to Abraham. God would remain with Jacob, provide for him, and protect him as he worked out his covenant promises. Jacob could continue his journey confident that God would secure his future.

**Literary Context.** Bereft of his inheritance and blessing—the two prerogatives of the eldest son—Esau was enraged. His only—misguided—solace was knowing that his father was nearing the end of his life. Once Isaac died, Esau could avenge himself by killing Jacob. Learning of

Esau's intention, Rebekah moved to protect her favorite son by persuading Isaac to send Jacob to her family in Haran to find a wife. But instead of simply telling Isaac about Esau's plan, she brought up the issue of Esau's marriages to two Hittite women (Gen 26:34).

In the ancient world, people commonly married within their own families or clans to preserve the family inheritance (see "Setting the Stage" in Chapter 1). By marrying Hittite women, Esau showed disregard for his parents and his heritage. Rebekah could have voiced her disgust over Esau's marriages at any time—they most likely occurred some years before the events of Genesis 27—but she chose to raise the issue now, voicing her fear that Jacob would also marry a Canaanite woman. Instead of accusing Isaac's favored son of ill will and voicing her concern for Jacob's safety (Gen 27:42–45), Rebekah appealed to a past grievance that she and Isaac shared (Gen 26:35; 27:46). In doing so, she shifted any blame for Jacob's move away from herself, suggesting that Esau's wives were the reason for his move, not her own recent deception. Once again, she manipulated Isaac into doing her will.

While Jacob's life began and ended in the land of promise, his flight from the house of his father signals more than a change in geography (Gen 25:19–35:29). Rebekah had planned for Jacob to stay with Laban "a few days" (Gen 27:44), but he would spend the next 20 years in exile from the promised land. In Genesis 28, he leaves for Haran at Rebekah's bidding and with Isaac's blessing, and he will not return to Canaan until Genesis 33.

These years in exile are bookended by two divine appointments. In Genesis 28, Jacob encountered the God of his fathers for the first time, and in Genesis 32, he will met him again. This technique to set off a section of the Bible with similar events helps draw our focus to what takes place in between the accounts.

> **Quick Bit:** Beginning and ending a section with a similar word, phrase, or concept is a common stylistic device in the OT called an *inclusio*. Psalm 118 shows a clear example of this technique.

In the time between Jacob's two direct encounters with him, God was at work in the life of Jacob the deceiver, confronting his flaws while prospering him in fulfillment of his original promises to Abraham.

**Historical & Cultural Background.** On Jacob's way to Haran, God spoke to him in a dream (Gen 28:12-15). When he awoke, he exclaimed, "Surely the LORD is in this place" (Gen 28:16 ESV). In the ancient Near East, people commonly thought of deities as tied to specific locations. Jacob's shock may reveal that he thought the God of his father was tied to Beersheba, where his father lived.

The concept of local deities is evident throughout the OT. When Assyria besieged Jerusalem during the reign of Hezekiah, the Assyrian commander boasted that he had defeated the gods of all the other nations (2 Kgs 19:12). After the conquest of Canaan, Joshua offered the people the choice between serving the local gods or Yahweh, who brought them out of Egypt (Josh 24:15-18). This understanding of the locality of deities is what leads the Syrian commander Naaman to request two mule-loads of dirt from Israel (2 Kgs 5:17). Naaman wanted soil from Israel so he could worship Israel's God in Syria.

After God appeared to him, Jacob made a vow that was conditional on God remaining with him. God would later identify himself to Jacob as the "the God of Bethel" (Gen 31:13), and Jacob would worship again at this location (Gen 35:1). God was not limited to Beer-sheba or Bethel. As Jacob would later acknowledge, God would be with him wherever he went (Gen 35:3) — even when he settled in Egypt, where God would make him into a great nation (Gen 46:2-4).

## A CLOSER LOOK

Jacob's schemes for dominance backfired. Although he now possessed the birthright and blessing of the eldest son, his conniving behavior had a consequence: his brother's wrath. As Jacob fled for his life, his prospects looked grim. Jacob had become a man without a country, family, or function. He had left everything behind in Beer-sheba. As he moved toward an uncertain future in Haran, he must have wondered, would the God of his ancestors follow him to this unfamiliar land?

In the opening verses of Genesis 28, Isaac bid his younger son farewell with instructions to find himself a wife from Rebekah's family. Before Jacob embarked on his journey, Isaac blessed him for a second time (Gen 28:3-4). The patriarch's words echo God's original blessing of creation (Gen 1:22, 28) as he asked God to bless Jacob by making him fruitful and multiplying him into a company of people. He then designated Jacob heir of God's promise to give Abraham and his descendants a land, to make them into a great nation, and to bless them and the world through them. Nearly every phrase repeats words of blessing given to both Abraham and Isaac (compare Gen 12:2-3, 7; 15:7-8; 26:3-4). In the events that follow, God would confirm Jacob's role as heir to the promise, though Jacob would receive his words with less than wholehearted acceptance.

> **Quick Bit:** The word "behold" is the Hebrew word *hinneh*. It is often used to signal a change in perspective or to indicate surprise.

After a long day of travel, Jacob stopped to spend the night in a place unknown to him. The sun set and, all alone, Jacob took a stone for a pillow, fell asleep, and dreamed vividly. We're invited to view the dream from Jacob's perspective: "Behold (*hinneh*), a stairway was set on the earth, and its top touched the heavens. And behold, angels of God were going up and going down on it. And behold, Yahweh was standing beside him" (Gen 28:12-13). Many English translations describe Yahweh as remaining at the top of the ladder or stairway, not beside Jacob. The Hebrew words can be understood either way, but Jacob's later statement "Surely Yahweh is indeed in this place" (Gen 28:16) suggests that Yahweh was standing on earth and not looking down from heaven. Yahweh's astounding presence and words of promise prove to Jacob that "earth is not left to its own resources and heaven is not a remote self-contained realm for the gods. Heaven has to do with earth. And earth finally may count on the resources of heaven."[1] This is exactly what the exiled Jacob needed to hear.

> **Quick Bit:** Jacob's ladder had a similar function as a ziggurat, a stepped temple tower in Mesopotamia that the ancients believed served as a gateway for the gods as they traveled between heaven and earth. In Jacob's dream, Yahweh himself came to earth to assure Jacob of his presence with him wherever he went.

Yahweh's words to Jacob take us to the central message of the passage. The God of Abraham and Isaac reaffirmed his covenant with the patriarchs' descendant and made five promises to Jacob. First, he included him in the covenant made with Abraham, promising him the land of Canaan, descendants as numerous as the dust of the earth, and a nation that would bless the whole world (Gen 12:1–3; 17:4–8). Next, he repeated to Jacob a promise he first made to Isaac: "I am with you" (compare Gen 26:3, 24). Then he made three new promises, which are of particular significance to a man on the run: He would protect Jacob wherever he went, he would bring him back to the land of promise, and he would not abandon him or his promises. These three promises should have offered Jacob the comfort and confidence he needed as he moved into his new life. But even they would not be enough for this reluctant patriarch.

**Quick Bit:** Jacob's encounter with God is an OT theophany, an appearance of God. The word "theophany" comes from two Greek words: *theos*, meaning "God," and *phainein*, meaning "to appear."

Jacob awakened and burst out, "Surely Yahweh is indeed in this place and I did not know!" (Gen 28:13). His words reveal surprise that his father's God, Yahweh, was not only in Beer-sheba, but also in this unknown place. He knew enough to be afraid, but he was not yet ready to accept this God as his God, as his actions reveal. Jacob took the rock he had been using as a pillow and set it up as a pillar to commemorate the event and mark the significance of the place. But he did not build an altar and worship the God in whose house he had just spent the night. By contrast, Abram built an altar and worshiped Yahweh as soon as he arrived in the land of promise (Gen 12:7; compare 12:8; 13:18), and Isaac built an altar when Yahweh extended his covenant with Abraham to him (Gen 26:25). Jacob won't build an altar until years later, when he returns to Bethel and acknowledges that God has kept his promises (Gen 35: 1–7).

Jacob's words also show that he hadn't yet embraced Yahweh as his God. In response to Yahweh's promise, Jacob offered a conditional bargain and vowed to make Yahweh his God *if*—and only *if*—he fulfilled Jacob's expectations. Jacob first required that Yahweh do what he had just said he would do: be with Jacob, protect him, and bring him back to the land. But these more abstract promises weren't enough for Jacob, who then specified that Yahweh must also provide his food and clothing.

When Jacob left Beer-sheba, he left everything behind—except his need to control his circumstances. And although he encountered Yahweh at Bethel, he didn't yet know him or trust him. It will take years in exile to pry Jacob's fingers off the controls of his life. The manipulator will meet his match in his future father-in-law, Laban, and come to realize that God takes care of him far better than he can take care of himself. In Laban's house, Jacob will grow wealthy in both people and possessions because God is caring for him and prospering him—in spite of his circumstances and situation.

# THROUGHOUT THE BIBLE

En route to Haran, Jacob spent the night in a place he named Bethel, "the house of God" (Gen 28:19), because he encountered Yahweh there. Years earlier, Abraham had camped near Bethel (Gen 12:8, 13:3) and built altars to Yahweh, the God who had brought him to Canaan and then preserved his life during famine.

Long after the time of the patriarchs, Bethel continued to play a significant role in the Israelites' experience. The Israelites, like Abraham before them, camped near Bethel on the eve of their second attack on the nearby city of Ai (Josh 8:3, 12). In Joshua's allotment of territory to the tribes after the conquest of Canaan, Bethel fell to Benjamin, though its location put it right on the border between Ephraim and Benjamin (Josh 16:1–2; 18:13). In the book of Judges, the border city of Bethel served as the gathering place for the Israelite troops attacking their kinsmen, the Benjaminites, after their heinous acts against the concubine in Judges 19 (compare Judg 20:18–48; 21:2, 19). Then, during the last days of the judges (before Israel had a king), Samuel traveled a circuit from Bethel to Gilgal and Mizpah, arbitrating differences between the people of Israel, calling them to faithful worship, and praying for their deliverance from the Philistines (1 Sam 7:5–16; compare 1 Sam 7:1–3).

> **Quick Bit:** Genesis 12:8 and 13:3 refer to Bethel at a time before Jacob actually changed the name of Luz to Bethel (Gen 28:19). Sometimes the biblical authors used later, more familiar names to refer to places so their audience would know what they were talking about.

Because of its central location and historical significance, Bethel was an early place of worship for the Israelites (1 Sam 10:3). However, after the construction of Solomon's temple, Jerusalem became the centralized place of worship, and the Israelites traveled to the temple there for national feasts throughout the year. When the kingdom split under Solomon's son, Rehoboam, the first king of the new northern kingdom feared divided loyalties if the northern tribes had to travel 10 miles south to Jerusalem to worship. So Jeroboam first exploited the religious tradition associated with Bethel and created an alternative for his people (1 Kgs 12:26–30): He set up golden calves in the border cities of Dan in the north and Bethel in the south for the people to worship.

Jeroboam's call to idolatry-based worship echoes the nearly verbatim call of Aaron (Moses' brother) at Mount Sinai. At Mount Sinai, Aaron fashioned a golden calf for the people to worship in the face of the apparent demise of their leader, Moses, atop the mountain (Exod 32:4, 8). Both Aaron and Jeroboam invited the people to worship the gods (or god) who brought them out of Egypt—the defining epithet of Yahweh after the exodus (Exod 12:17; Lev 11:45; Num 15:41; Deut 5:6). While both leaders may have believed they were calling the people to worship Yahweh in an alternative way, their blatant violation of the commandment to make no graven images meant they led their people into idolatry instead. Jeroboam's perversion of worship at Bethel becomes the damning sin of the northern kingdom (2 Kgs 10:29; Hos 10:15; Amos 3:14). The "house of God," where Yahweh made his covenant with Jacob, instead became what the prophet Hosea called the "house of wickedness" (*Beth-aven*; Hos 4:15; 10:5; compare Amos 5:5).

## BEYOND THE BIBLE

The extraordinary image of the ladder to heaven from Genesis 28:10–17 has had a lasting effect on religious thought, art, and literature. A ladder with angels ascending and descending on it was so striking that interpreters were certain that some symbolic message lay behind it. The ancient symbolism of the ziggurat (a stepped pyramid symbolizing the place where heaven and earth meet) was long forgotten, so the meaning of the ladder was spiritualized or allegorized. Philo of Alexandria explained how the ladder represented the highs and lows of a life of virtue.[2]

> But the practisers of virtue, for they are on the boundary between two extremities, are frequently going upwards and downwards as if on a ladder, being either drawn upwards by a more powerful fate, or else being dragged down by that which is worse; until the umpire of this contention and conflict, namely God, adjudges the victory to the more excellent class and utterly destroys the other (Philo, *De Somniis* 1.152).

In Philo's view, righteous people are like Jacob at the "gate of heaven." They're in a transitional state, caught between heaven and earth, pulled toward heaven or hell depending on the quality of their deeds. In this interpretation, God's favor and our salvation are based on our deeds.

> **Quick Bit:** Philo of Alexandria (20 BC– AD 50) was a Jewish philosopher living in the Hellenistic (Greek) city of Alexandria in Egypt. His most well-known writings are interpretations of the OT, especially the Pentateuch. Philo's method blended traditional Jewish interpretation with Greek philosophical concepts. He was also especially fond of allegorical interpretation.

Other interpreters view the ladder to heaven as assurance of God's continual presence. The church father John Chysostom (ca. AD 347-407) focused on how Jacob's dream demonstrated God's love for Jacob, even to the point of identifying Christ's involvement in the story:

> Notice here, I ask you, the extraordinary care of the loving God. When he saw [Jacob] consenting to the journey in accordance with his mother's advice, which came out of fear of his brother, and taking to the road like some athlete, with no support from any source, leaving everything instead to help from on high, Christ wanted at the very beginning of the journey to strengthen Jacob's resolve. And so he appeared to him with the words "I am the God of Abraham and the God of your father Isaac. I have caused the patriarch and your father to experience a great increase in prosperity; so, far from being afraid, believe that I am he who fulfilled my promises and will shower on you my care."[3]

In Jacob, we find a reluctant patriarch—one hesitant to acknowledge God's sovereignty and place trust in him. But through his story, we encounter a God who cares for his people, blesses them, and keeps his promises.

Jacob had long heard of God's astonishing works in the lives of his ancestors. Now, he would experience God's presence firsthand as God met him in his time of need and extended to him the promise he had made to Abraham and Isaac.

## APPLICATION

Unlike Abraham, whose faith carried him to an unknown land, Jacob fled to a faraway place to escape a dangerous situation his own misdeeds had created. When the God of heaven approached him at Bethel—declaring promises of protection, blessing, and prosperity—Jacob was in awe, but he still wasn't ready to trust him. It's one thing to hear about what God can do; it's another to experience it in our own lives. Jacob responded to God's generous promises with a deal: God, if you will do *this*, then I will let you be my God.

What Jacob didn't yet realize was that God will be God, regardless of whether we "let" him. Jacob liked to hold the reins to his life, and his grip was unyielding. So the longsuffering God of Abraham and Isaac took Jacob on a long journey of letting go. As everything comfortable and familiar crumbled around him, Jacob would learn that God can indeed be trusted.

Many of us find a kindred spirit in Jacob. We understand his reluctance to embrace God's promises. After all, we just never know what God might do if we yield control of our lives. But the Bible affirms again and again that God—and *only* God—can be trusted. Any trust we place in human strength or ability, including our own, is misplaced (Psa 20:7; Prov 3:5–6; Isa 31:1). Human resources are limited. People will disappoint us. Our own strength will fail. But as Jacob would learn, God is unable to fail.

# DISCUSSION

## A Closer Look

1. What does Jacob's conditional vow with God say about his faith? Have you made similar conditional promises to God? What was the situation?

_____

_____

_____

2. God reached out to Jacob when he was in a difficult situation. Have you felt God reaching out to you during a trying time? How did you experience God's protection or provision?

_____

_____

_____

## Throughout the Bible

1. How do Christians today make "graven images" that they substitute for true worship of God, perhaps without realizing it?

_____

_____

_____

2. Can you think of other times in the Bible when God's people turned something sacred or special into something idolatrous? How do we do this today?

_____

_____

_____

**Beyond the Bible**

1. Reflect on one way that God demonstrates his extraordinary care for you.

_____

_____

_____

2. How can the image of a ladder or stairway symbolize the Christian life as we move closer or farther away from being Christlike?

_____

_____

_____

**Application**

1. Have you ever been reluctant to trust God about something? What was it, and why did you have such a difficult time letting go?

_____

_____

_____

2. Can you think of a time when you trusted God to take care of something and he proved himself beyond your expectations? Did that make it easier to trust him again for something else?

_____

_____

_____

## CHAPTER 4

# HIRED HELP

*Read Genesis 29:1–35; 30:1–24.*

## SETTING THE STAGE

**Theme.** We find great encouragement in hearing about God's mighty acts in the past—the ways in which he intervened, delivered, and provided for his people. But at the same time, reading of his vivid presence in the past can lead us to wonder, "Where is God now? What's he done for us today?" Understanding how God works in and through his people requires balance—remembering what he did throughout history and recognizing what he's doing now.

Jacob had long heard about the mighty God of his ancestors, but to Jacob, God remained just that—the God of his *ancestors*. Jacob wanted God to prove himself, to fulfill his end of their bargain (Gen 28:20-22). Although God had appeared to Jacob in a dream and promised to bless him, Jacob remained blinded by his own self-centeredness and personal ambitions.

Despite Jacob's refusal to recognize God's hand, God was at work, giving Jacob children and thus keeping the promises he made to Abraham (Gen 12:2-3). And through it all, God was preparing Jacob for a time when he would fully recognize his presence.

**Literary Context.** The opening events of the story of Jacob's exile in Haran echo the earlier story of Abraham's servant finding a wife for Isaac (Gen 24). Like Abraham's servant before him, Jacob arrived at the well, where he encountered a woman related to Laban, Abraham's relative.[1] Like Abraham's servant, Jacob was then greeted by Laban and welcomed into his home. Yet there are some striking differences between the two accounts. Abraham's servant had arrived with a caravan of gifts in tow; Jacob was penniless and alone. Abraham's servant took Rebekah away from the house of her brother, Laban; Jacob will become part of Laban's household. But perhaps most significantly, Abraham's servant implored God to help him; Jacob, despite his vulnerable position, didn't seem to give God a second thought.

As Jacob's stay in Haran continued, an ironic role reversal turns the deceiver into the deceived. Jacob had tricked his father, Isaac, into blessing him instead of Esau. Now, Laban will deceive Jacob on his wedding night, giving him his older daughter Leah for a wife. When Jacob implored, "What is this you have done to me? ... Now why did you deceive me?" Laban fired back with words that should have pierced Jacob: "It is not the custom in our country to give the younger before the firstborn" (Gen 29:26).

In the ensuing events, we unearth one additional theme that ties Jacob's story into the larger Genesis narrative: The idea of "seed" or "descendants." This theme permeates the book of Genesis, beginning in the account of creation (Gen 1:11-12) and continuing through the genealogical records of Genesis 5 and 10. In Genesis 12, 15, and 17, descendants are a key part of God's promise to Abraham. Thus far in Genesis, however, the viability of the promise has repeatedly been in doubt. Abraham's wife was barren and aged. Their miracle son, Isaac, survived a near-death experience at the hands of his own father, but then he married a woman who also proved barren. With God's intervention, Rebekah bore Jacob and Esau, but subsequent strife threatened to destroy the entire family. Thus far, the line of promised descendants has been tenuous at best, seemingly one breath away from extinction. But during Jacob's exile in Haran, the family line would take root. By the time the patriarch returned to the land of promise, he would have 11 sons and a daughter. Later, when Jacob's descendants were enslaved in Egypt, God would continue to bless his chosen people with offspring, growing 12 families into a nation.

**Historical & Cultural Background.** Family strife seemed to accompany Jacob wherever he went. Estranged from his own brother, Jacob introduced tension into the lives of the sisters he married, Leah and Rachel. Just as Jacob's own parents showed blatant favoritism, Jacob couldn't conceal his preference for Rachel. A battle for Jacob's affection ensued between the sisters.

> **Quick Bit:** While many men in the Bible had more than one wife, and the Mosaic law regulated polygynous households (those in which a man had more than one wife; Exod 21:10–11; Lev 18:18; Deut 21:15–16), the OT does not endorse the practice. God never commands any man to take another wife. Several biblical narratives even hinge on the rivalries and other problems that result from polygyny, such as that of Hagar and Sarah, showing how destructive such relationships can be.

For Jacob's wives, rivalry took the form of providing Jacob with the most offspring. This competition reflects the importance of descendants in the ancient Near East. Children—especially sons—guaranteed both the immediate and long-term survival of a family. In an agrarian subsistence culture, children helped support the family by working in the fields, caring for animals, and helping run the household (Gen 29:6–9; 1 Sam 16:11; 2 Kgs 4:18–20). When a girl married, her husband paid her father a bride price to compensate for the loss of the daughter's labor. But the value of sons was inestimable. In addition to their economic worth, male descendants were heirs who would care for parents in their old age, maintain the inheritance, and continue the family line. Males trained throughout their lives to eventually assume operation of the family business.

When God made his covenant with Abraham, he promised to bless him and the entire world through him (Gen 12:1–3). This blessing included fertility—that is, Abraham would father many nations, and one of those nations, Israel, would be a means by which God would bless the whole earth. God later made a covenant with Israel in which he promised perpetual fertility if they kept his commandments: "Blessed will be the fruit of your womb and the fruit of your ground and the fruit of your livestock, the calf of your cattle and the lambs of your flock" (Deut 28:4). God's intent for his covenant people was that they would show the world what a blessed life looked like—and in doing so, they would draw the nations to God.

Conversely, Israel's disobedience to the covenant would bring barrenness: "The fruit of your womb *shall* be cursed and the fruit of your ground, the calves of your cattle and the lambs of your flock" (Deut 28:18). When the people disobeyed the covenant, the prophets drew on imagery of infertility and barrenness to indict them for their sin. Isaiah warned that Israel would be a desolate, ravaged vineyard (Isa 5:1–7), and Hosea compared the nation to a barren woman (Hos 9:11–17).

For this reason, barrenness was more than just an unfortunate situation. In ancient Israel, a barren woman was also stigmatized socially since childbearing reflected God's blessing (Gen 1:28; Exod 23:26). In addition, childbearing fulfilled the promises God made to Abraham (Gen 12:1–3). Women went to extreme lengths to overcome barrenness, as we can see in Sarah's actions with Hagar (Gen 16). Barrenness may also explain why Hannah's husband, Elkanah, had a second wife (1 Sam 1).

In their battle for children, Jacob's wives employed mandrakes. In the ancient world, plants that resembled the human body were believed to have magical powers to heal those body parts. Since the mandrake is a plant with forked roots resembling a human figure, it had a reputation for aiding human fertility.[2] But the story of Leah and Rachel dismisses any notion that the mandrakes had power. Leah gave up the fertility plants and then conceived two sons in succession, while Rachel, who used the mandrakes, remained infertile. Through these women's lives, God displays that he alone will grant children and that he is the power his people should rely on.

> **Quick Bit:** In the ancient Near East, people commonly employed magic to access the knowledge and power of the supernatural world. They used methods of divination to obtain that knowledge, and they used magic to coax supernatural powers into influencing the natural world.

## A CLOSER LOOK

After Jacob received assurances of God's promises during his divine encounter at Bethel (Gen 28), he arrived in the "land of the Easterners" (Gen 29:1). This vague expression might indicate that Jacob didn't quite know where he was, nor how close he might be to Haran where Laban, his mother's brother, lived. He happened upon a well, where he found three flocks of sheep and their shepherds, who were waiting for other local shepherds to arrive. Together, they could roll the large stone away from the well and water all the sheep.

When Jacob asked the shepherds where they were from, he must have been thrilled and relieved by their response: "Haran." What's more, they knew Laban, the very person he was seeking. While the men talked, Rachel, the lone shepherdess, arrived. When Jacob saw her, he was overcome. He singlehandedly hefted the large stone from the well to water his uncle's flocks, and then, kissing Rachel, he wept. Only later we will learn that Rachel was beautiful (Gen 29:17), but Jacob's emotion here derives from her being the daughter of "Laban his mother's brother"—a fact we hear three times in one verse (Gen 29:10). This repetition links Rachel to Isaac and Rebekah's instructions (Gen 27:43; 28:2), hinting to us that Rachel will be the wife Jacob has come to find. This three-fold repetition may also be a clue that Laban will turn out to be very much like Jacob's mother. We know Rebekah as a schemer, manipulator, and deceiver. It won't take long for Laban to prove they are related. Rebekah's plotting put Jacob in Haran, and Laban's will keep him there.

> **Quick Bit:** Repetition is a technique of biblical storytelling that can draw our attention to important ideas in the story. Some translations smooth out repetition to make a more appealing English reading, so it is helpful to use a translation that preserves the repetition of the original Hebrew.

Finding his relatives after such a long, lonely journey reduced Jacob to tears. Rachel ran to tell her father about the man at the well, and, as he had done years earlier when Abraham's servant arrived at the well, Laban rushed out to meet the stranger. But Jacob was not like Abraham's servant—a fact Laban recognized immediately—and there would be no lavish gifts in exchange for a bride this time. Jacob had come to find a wife, but he had nothing to offer in return. Despite Jacob's circumstances, Laban welcomed him into his household.

After Jacob had stayed and worked with Laban for a month—during which Laban observed his nephew's infatuation with Rachel—Laban seized an opportunity to exploit Jacob's situation. His offer of a job sounds innocent enough to us, but Laban effectively demoted his own "flesh and bone" (Gen 29:14) to a hireling in his house. Although Isaac had blessed Jacob and said others would serve him (Gen 27:29; compare 25:23; 27:37, 40), Jacob will instead serve another man—his own uncle—for 20 years. This story drives home the irony of Jacob's situation by using the word *serve* (*abad*) seven times (Gen 29:15, 18, 20, 25, 27, 30).

At the end of his seven years of service, Jacob insisted that Laban give him Rachel, the wife he had earned. We don't know exactly how Laban managed to trick Jacob into sleeping with the wrong woman, but it was dark, Leah was likely veiled, and Jacob was quite possibly drunk. Sober in the morning, Jacob was horrified to discover what Laban had done. But when he accused Laban of deception, he also indicted himself for his own deception years earlier. Jacob had met his match.

Jacob wouldn't have to wait another seven years to marry Rachel. Laban would happily allow Jacob to marry her now—and work for another seven years in return (Gen 29:28). Smitten with Rachel, Jacob agreed with apparently no hesitation. The text indicates he married her right away (Gen 29:29)—but he was bound to an oath to continue working for Laban. He would continue to be a servant even though he was an heir of a great promise. The oath Jacob made prevented him, for seven years, from returning to the land God promised to Abraham. Nonetheless, being one to avoid conflict whenever possible, Jacob probably doesn't mind not returning to reclaim the land promised to Abraham—and now him—because that would involve dealing with Esau. Genesis 29:30 states clearly the situation between the two sisters and their shared husband: "[Jacob] loved Rachel more than Leah." Rachel was beautiful and loved. Leah was the leftover daughter Laban hoodwinked Jacob into marrying. The circumstance echoes that of Jacob and Esau, where Rebekah "loved Jacob," while Esau—the rightful heir and older son—is loved by his father, Isaac (Gen 25:28).

The unloved Leah attracted the attention of Yahweh, who opened her womb. Leah gave her first three sons names that express her despair: Reuben, because "Yahweh has noticed my misery" (Gen 29:32); Simeon, because "Yahweh has heard that I am unloved" (Gen 29:33); and Levi, because "this time my husband will be joined to me" (Gen 29:34). Only at the birth of her fourth son, Judah, did Leah resign herself to her fate: "This time I will praise Yahweh" (Gen 29:35). She could not win her husband's love, and her misery increased, but she would still praise God.

> **Quick Bit:** Many names in the OT are theophoric, meaning they contain a divine name or title as part of a larger sentence. The name Yahweh often appears in partial form in English as *jeho-* or *jo-* (Jehoshaphat, "Yahweh has judged"; Jonathan, "Yahweh has given") or *-iah* (Isaiah, "Yahweh is salvation"). The title God, Hebrew *'el*, is also used this way (Daniel, "God is my judge"). These attributions to Yahweh recognized his hand in people's lives, and often foretold the type of people they would be or the events or issues they would have to confront.

Leah was fertile, but Rachel, the wife who held Jacob's heart, was barren. Despondent after watching Leah bear son after son, Rachel lashed out at Jacob and demanded children. In his retort, Jacob shifted the blame away from himself: "Am I in the place of God, who has withheld from you the fruit of the womb?" (Gen 30:2). This response wasn't good enough for Rachel, who, in an act reminiscent of Sarah (Jacob's grandmother), instructed Jacob to sleep with Bilhah, her servant (compare Gen 16). Bilhah then bore two sons for Rachel to claim as her own. With the birth of Naphtali ("I have struggled a mighty struggle with my sister and have prevailed," Gen 30:8) Rachel thought she had gained the upper hand over her fertile sister. Not to be outdone, Leah gave her own servant, Zilpah, to Jacob, and Zilpah also had two sons, Gad and Asher. But neither woman was happy. Each still desperately wanted what the other had: Leah wanted Jacob's love, and Rachel wanted to bear his children.

Things go from bad to worse for the unloved Leah, who, in spite of having given Jacob six sons, has to bargain with Rachel to sleep with her own husband. When Reuben presents his mother, Leah, with the mandrake roots, Rachel politely asks for some. Leah bites back, accusing Rachel of taking her husband and then also demanding her mandrakes. Rachel struck a bargain with Leah: a night with Jacob in exchange for some mandrakes. Leah readily agreed to the deal and conceived during her night with Jacob. She then bore a son, and later she gave birth to another son and a daughter. And despite the mandrakes, Rachel remained barren. Finally "God remembered Rachel and listened to her, and God opened her womb" (Gen 30:22). At the birth of Joseph, the long-awaited child, Rachel declared that God had taken away her disgrace.

Throughout his wives' bitter rivalry, Jacob stood by silently, unwilling to intervene. He was a passive husband, and he would also be a passive father, doing little during the later incident at Shechem (Gen 34) and ignoring the animosity between his favorite son, Joseph, and the rest of his sons (Gen 37). His failure to act brought great strife to his family.

## THROUGHOUT THE BIBLE

Rachel's barrenness vividly portrays the fallen state of humanity. Fertility for both land and people was God's design for his creation (Gen 1:11–12, 28). Yet when Adam and Eve sinned, their action brought God's curse on human fertility and the fruitfulness of the land they cared for (Gen 3:16–19). Only with great effort would people coax the land to produce, and only in great pain and even danger would women birth children. The fruitful blessedness of creation gave way to the desolate consequences of sin.

Rachel is one of six women in the Bible whose barrenness God overcomes. The stories of these women and their miracle sons weave a story of God's redemptive power to bring life from death.

The Bible's first barren woman is Sarah, Abraham's wife (Gen 11:30). At the very headwaters of God's redemptive plan to bless the fallen world stood a barren woman. It would take a miracle for God to even begin to keep his promise, but he did it. From the barren womb of Sarah, God brought the son of promise, Isaac.

Sarah's successor, Rebekah, was also barren (Gen 25:21), but through the prayers of her husband, Isaac, Rebekah birthed twins. Jacob, the younger son, came out fighting for his own way, and he kept at it for much of his life. Renamed Israel, he was an appropriate namesake for the nation that would also fight stubbornly for its own way.

Like her two matriarchal predecessors, Rachel was barren (Gen 29:31) until God opened her womb with Joseph. It was through this long-awaited son and the adverse circumstances of his life as a captive in Egypt that

God preserved the fledgling tribes of Israel during the years of severe famine in Canaan.

After Rachel, barren women disappear from the biblical story until the desperate days of the judges. When enemies of Israel threatened to destroy them, God visited the barren wife of Manoah and promised a son that would deliver the people (Judg 13:2–23). Through Samson's supernatural strength, God protected the Israelites from their archenemies, the Philistines.

At the end of the period of the judges, barren Hannah pleaded for a son, whom she promised to give back to God (1 Sam 1:2, 5, 11). God raised up Samuel to speak his word and intercede for his people in those dark days when people who spoke the word of Yahweh were rare (1 Sam 3:1).

The sixth barren woman in the Bible is Elizabeth, the mother of John the Baptist (Luke 1:7). Her story echoes that of the first barren woman, Sarah, who was also long past the years of childbearing. Her son, was the voice calling in the wilderness to prepare people for the coming of the Messiah.

This block of stories culminates in the story of a miraculous birth from "innocent barrenness," the virgin womb of Mary. While each son of a barren woman played an important role in the life of historic Israel, each also pointed to the Savior who was to come, Jesus. Isaac foreshadowed the perfect sacrifice of Jesus on the cross, but unlike Isaac, Jesus *was* the provided lamb. Jacob had 12 sons who formed the foundation for the national people of Israel, but Jesus chose 12 men as the foundation of a new people of God that transcends ethnic boundaries. The cruel mistreatment Joseph suffered at the hands of his brothers paved the way for their eventual rescue from certain death; Jesus' suffering and death at the hands of his "brothers" (his people) made a way for all people to be rescued from certain death. Samson delivered the nation of Israel from the Philistines for a season, but Jesus has delivered us from sin's bondage forever. Samuel was the first prophet in an era of men and women who proclaimed Yahweh's words to the people of Israel, but Jesus was the fullness of God's Word for all people for all time. John the Baptist insisted that his message only prepared the way for one greater than himself: Jesus.

Jesus' life, death, and resurrection were God's final provision for the human condition of spiritual barrenness. Jesus broke the hold of sin and death, the barrenness of human existence, and offers the fullness of life that God intended for his creation from the beginning. The story of the Bible ends with the image of a flourishing, fruitful city and a beautiful bride (the Church, being God's people) prepared for her husband (Jesus). Barrenness will be gone forever.

## BEYOND THE BIBLE

Jacob's tentative faith was apparent to early biblical interpreters, who noted a fundamental difference between the barrenness of Sarah and Rebekah and that of Rachel. In Genesis 30:1, Rachel pleaded with Jacob to give her children, but Jacob angrily turned the focus to God, blaming him for "with[holding] from you [Rachel] the fruit of the womb" (Gen 30:2). On the surface, this excuse aligns with what Genesis says elsewhere about barrenness (e.g., Gen 16:2), but the church father Ephrem suggested that perhaps Jacob shared some of the blame:

> Leah bore Reu-ben, Simeon, Levi and Judah and then ceased giving birth, whereas Rachel was barren. Because she heard Jacob say that Abraham had prayed over the barren Sarah and was heard and that Isaac had also prayed for Rebekah and was answered, she thought that it was because Jacob had not prayed for her that her closed womb had not been opened. For this reason, she said in anger and in tears, "Give me children, or I shall die!"[3]

Ephrem emphasizes how Isaac had prayed for Rebekah (Gen 25:21) and attributes the same care to Abraham (Gen 15:6). The real cause of Rachel's barrenness, then, could be Jacob's lack of faith. Abraham believed, Isaac prayed, but Jacob made excuses.

**Quick Bit:** Ephrem (AD 306-373) was the most prolific writer in Syriac Christianity. He became a monk and taught in the cities of Nisibis and Edessa in northwestern Mesopotamia. Ephrem wrote sermons, hymns, theological treatises, and biblical commentaries. His commentary on Genesis is one of his most well-known works, authored in the ancient language of Syriac.

Ephrem's suggestion provides a relevant context for Rachel's contentious confrontation with Jacob. She was motivated by piety, not just envy over her sister's success. Maybe she was barren because Jacob hadn't interceded on her behalf before God. Then again, maybe that wouldn't have helped.

Where Rachel saw injustice, it seems that the narrator of Genesis sees divinely appointed poetic justice. Since Leah was hated while Rachel was loved, God opened the womb of the unloved wife to compensate for her loveless marriage (Gen 29:31–35). This was certainly Leah's own view of events based on her response when each of her four sons was born. Unfortunately, Leah's greatest desire was to gain her husband's love, yet even her success at bearing children for him was not enough to draw him close. The church father John Chrysostom (ca. AD 347–407) explained God's intervention as a sort of balance of power between Leah and Rachel:

> Whereas one woman by her beauty attracted her husband's favor, the other seemed to be rejected because she lacked it. But it was the latter [Leah] God awoke to childbirth while leaving the other's [Rachel's] womb inactive. He thus dealt with each in his characteristic love so that one might have some comfort from what was born of her and the other might not triumph over her sister on the score of charm and beauty.[4]

Unlike with Rebekah and Sarah, Rachel's barrenness was not an obstacle to the continuation of the line of Abraham. Her fertility was a non-essential, so within Chrysostom's view, God blessed Leah instead. Chrysostom's view is favored by the descent of the two most prominent tribes in Israel's history from Leah—Judah and Levi, the tribe of kings and priests. Nonetheless, it's certain that Jacob's overall attitude affected his family life and that his aloof attitude toward God may have kept him from understanding the real reason why Rachel remained barren.

## APPLICATION

God was moving in Jacob's life, even though Jacob failed to recognize it. With each birth of a new child, Jacob could watch God literally fulfill his promise to make Abraham's heirs into a nation. But Jacob still had trouble believing that God was with him and providing for him. He had heard the stories of God's faithfulness to Abraham and Isaac, but he struggled to recognize God's hand in his own life.

Yet when Jacob faced the heartache of watching his most beloved wife, Rachel, struggle to conceive, he found it easy to identify the God of his fathers as the culprit. In the process, Jacob failed to acknowledge God's provision—except when he felt that God wasn't providing.

Jacob's flaws are hard to miss—skeptical, passive in conflict, and self-centered—but we're often eager to overlook them because we see his faults mirrored in ourselves. We understand why Jacob struggled to believe God was for him—sometimes we do, too. The Bible tells us how God intervened, delivered, and provided for his people in the past. When we experience the pain of our broken world, we wonder why he doesn't do the same for us. We crave tangible and obvious signs of his work in our lives. Yet Jesus reminds us that "Blessed are those who have not seen and have believed" (John 20:29). Even when God's hand isn't evident, we can be confident that he is at work in our lives, weaving our circumstances and talents into his greater design.

# DISCUSSION

**A Closer Look**

1. Have you experienced a time when you were unloved or rejected while someone else was preferred? How did you respond? How did you treat the other person?

_____

_____

_____

2. Have you ever been deceived like Jacob was? How did you respond? Did it cause you to reflect on times when you may have deceived others?

_____

_____

_____

**Throughout the Bible**

1. Why do you think the Bible has so many examples of barren women? What can their stories teach us about relying on God?

_____

_____

_____

2. What does barrenness (either of people or land) say about the earth? What do you think the "new heaven" and "new earth" (see Rev 21:1–4) will be like?

_____

_____

_____

**Beyond the Bible**

1. When things don't go our way, sometimes we look for a reason to explain why God's not blessing us like we think he should. Was there a time when you blamed yourself or someone else for something that was out of anyone's control?

_____

_____

_____

2. How do your own personal struggles prevent you from seeing the big picture of what God's doing around you?

_____

_____

_____

**Application**

1. How do the stories of God's faithfulness to his people in Scripture give you hope during times of trial?

_____

_____

_____

2. Do you feel like God is as present in your life as he was in the lives of the patriarchs—why or why not? What are some ways you can see God's presence in your life?

_____

_____

_____

## CHAPTER 5

# DUELING DECEIVERS

*Read Genesis 30:25–31:55.*

## SETTING THE STAGE

**Theme.** It seems like human nature to look out for ourselves—we're often driven by self-preservation and self-promotion. When we become new creations in Christ, this should change (2 Cor 5:17). Rather than pursuing our own interests, we should pursue what is important to God. We often fail in this. Most of us have a tendency to be self-interested, pursuing our own wants or trying to control every detail of our lives. Thankfully, even when we falter in our faithfulness to God, he remains perfect in his faithfulness to us.

Up until now, Jacob has primarily looked out for himself, pursuing his own interests. Even when he made an oath to God, it was conditional on his own needs being met (Gen 28:20–22). Yet as Jacob turned a blind eye to God's work in his life, God continued to bless him. When tensions between Jacob and Laban rose, God made Jacob profit at Laban's expense (Gen 31:9). As Jacob's prosperity became evident to even Laban and his sons, it all seemed to click for Jacob; he finally recognized that God had been with him all along (Gen 35:2–3). Despite Jacob's reluctant faith, God remained faithful.

**Literary Context.** It had been 14 years since Jacob fled to Haran to escape his brother and to find a wife (Gen 27:43–28:5). In that time, he had acquired 2 wives and had 12 children (11 sons and a daughter). Now, he was ready to return home. But for Jacob and his family to return to Canaan with anything more than the clothes on their backs, they would have to escape Laban. Jacob's years in Haran began and ended on notes of strife and deception.

It was Jacob's deception of his father, Isaac, that enraged his brother Esau and sent Jacob running for his life. He may have slipped through his brother's fingers, but Jacob ran headlong into his conniving uncle, Laban. Laban tricked Jacob into marrying both of his daughters—making him labor for an additional seven years for Rachel, the only wife Jacob wanted. When Jacob finally tried to leave his uncle, he knew he would have to outsmart him.

Strife and deception characterized Jacob's life in Haran as much as it did his life in Canaan. But God was with Jacob as he promised (Gen 28:15). When Jacob bargained with God at Bethel, he demanded that God provide his bread and clothing—the bare necessities for survival. But God did much more than Jacob asked. While Jacob was in Haran, God made him a rich man and gave him many children. As he promised, the God of Abraham and Isaac blessed their descendant, Jacob.

**Historical & Cultural Background.** When Jacob approached his uncle announcing that he was ready to take his family and return home, he didn't receive the response he had hoped for. Laban recognized that his household had prospered under Jacob's care, and he wasn't quite ready to let that go. So Jacob and Laban struck a deal: Jacob could have any sheep or goats that varied in color from the typical white for sheep and dark for goats (Gen 30:31–33).[1]

Jacob then took some unusual steps to multiply his flock: Peeling back the bark on fresh sticks of poplar, almond, and plane trees, he set up the striped pieces of wood at the troughs where the animals bred (Gen 30:37–39). The idea was that animals breeding in view of the striped sticks would produce mottled, speckled, and spotted young that Jacob could claim for his flock. Then, Jacob monitored which animals bred among the sticks so that only the strongest birthed discolored offspring (Gen 30:41–42).

Jacob's actions don't make much sense to us, but they were based on ancient Near Eastern beliefs about breeding. The thought was that whatever an animal saw while breeding could influence the offspring. Jacob made sure Laban's strong animals saw striped sticks so that the resulting offspring would have varied colors. Jacob acted out of beliefs similar to those of Rachel and Leah when they employed mandrakes in an attempt to conceive children (Gen 30:14–17; see "Setting the Stage" in Chapter 4).

From Genesis 30:43, we see that Jacob's plan worked, but there is no indication that it was because of his superstitious breeding methods. Instead, God was looking out for him. Jacob became "exceedingly rich and had large flocks, female slaves, male slaves, camels, and donkeys." Some scholars have offered scientific explanations for Jacob's prosperity in animal breeding,[2] but surprisingly out of character for him at this stage, Jacob attributed his success to the true source—God (Gen 31:6–12).

## A CLOSER LOOK

Haran was supposed to be a temporary escape from tensions back home. Now, 14 years, two wives, and 12 children later, the time had come for Jacob to return home. Approaching his uncle, he demanded that Laban let him go, taking his wives and children with him. Jacob had paid the bride prices for Leah and Rachel with his 14 years of service, but he was legally entitled to nothing else. Later law in Israel would require that when an employer releases a servant, he must send him off with resources to help him get on his feet (Deut 15:12–15), but we don't know if Haran had a similar law. As a son-in-law, Jacob might have hoped he would receive kinder treatment than just any employee, but he knew better. His demand appealed not to their kinsmen relationship, but to his service record. He wanted Laban to realize that he had worked hard enough in 14 years to earn not only his wives, but also his children and his freedom. Four times Jacob referred to his service (*avad*; Gen 30:26, 29), and then he reminded Laban that *he* was a wealthy man because of Jacob (Gen 30:29–30).

Laban didn't need the reminders. He was well aware of Jacob's economic value and had no intention of losing him—or, at least, the wealth he brought. So rather than answering Jacob's initial demand, he offered Jacob a bribe. Jacob didn't budge. He wanted to make a home for his family back in the land of promise. Laban persisted, so Jacob decided to take advantage of his uncle's desperate greed. He offered to continue shepherding

Laban's flock on the condition that he get his own starter flock, consisting of all the mottled, speckled, and spotted animals (Gen 39:31–33). Any future-born sheep or goats whose coloring varied from the typical white for sheep and dark for goats would also be his.

Given that the vast majority of sheep were white and most goats were dark,[3] Laban recognized a good deal when he saw one. Jacob was asking for less than the typical 20 percent shepherds would have received as wages.[4] But just in case the tricky Jacob had something up his sleeve, the trickier Laban removed the starter flock that Jacob should have had and relocated it three days' away from Jacob (Gen 39:32, 35).

Undaunted, Jacob implemented a new breeding program utilizing peeled sticks (see "Setting the Stage"). His plan worked: He became "exceedingly rich and had large flocks," (Gen 30:43). It is only later that Jacob acknowledged what's written between the lines of his strange strategy and burgeoning wealth. The unusual number of spotted and speckled animals born to Laban's flock was not on account of Jacob's genius—rather, God did it. God saw Laban's exploitation of Jacob, so he made Laban's flocks produce a surplus of mottled, speckled, and sturdy animals (Gen 31:6–12). Jacob drew them all into his flock, and God fulfilled his promise to bless Jacob.

While Jacob grew wealthy, Laban's sons grew resentful. Recognizing that even Laban seemed to dislike him (Gen 31:1–2), Jacob realized it was time to leave. When Yahweh confirmed his hunch, ordering him to depart (Gen 31:3), Jacob's mind was set. This time there would be no turning back, no negotiating with his uncle. Jacob called his wives together, and for the first time the descendant of Abraham and Isaac acknowledged God's hand in his life and credited him for his blessing (Gen 31:4–13). The bargaining refugee from Bethel finally embraced the God who met him there.

Hearing Jacob's impassioned words, Rachel and Leah stood in unison for the first time in the story. Laban had been a bad father as well as a rotten father-in-law, and Jacob's wives were ready to leave (Gen 31:14–16). The family packed up and fled, and when Laban heard, he hurried after them. Just outside the land of Canaan, the two deceivers came head to head.

Laban played the injured father: "What have you done that you tricked me and have carried off my daughters like captives of the sword? Why did you hide *your intention* to flee and trick me, and did not tell me so that I would have sent you away with joy and song and tambourine and lyre? And *why* did you not give me opportunity to kiss my grandsons and my daughters *goodbye*?" (Gen 31:26–28). The outraged Laban spewed one more accusation: As if all this weren't bad enough, "why did you steal my gods?" (Gen 39:30). Jacob, we learn, didn't steal the gods, but Rachel did—a fact Jacob did not know.

Jacob responded honestly. He was afraid Laban would send him off as he had arrived 20 years earlier, with nothing. Then he granted Laban permission to search the camp for his household gods and promised to kill whoever might have them. Laban ransacked the family's tents in his futile hunt for the gods that Rachel (feigning menstruation) was sitting on (Gen 31:35). When Laban came up empty handed, the patient submission that Jacob had demonstrated for 20 years was spent. He unleashed his anger and frustration on father-in-law, declaring that he had prospered only because God had been on his side (Gen 31:36–42).

Laban returned fire and showed what a scoundrel he really was. He waved his hand over Jacob's entourage and claimed it all belonged to him: the daughters, the flocks, and the children (Gen 31:43). He knew his words were unfounded, so he quickly attempted to save face by inviting Jacob to make a treaty with him (Gen 31:44). The two men heaped stones together and agreed that, with God as their witness, they would stay away from each other (Gen 31:45–50).

> **Quick Bit:** Laban and Jacob made their treaty at Mizpah. Their words, "The Lord watch between you and me, when we are out of one another's sight," have often been used to affirm friendships or even marriages. However, in their original context, the words called for separation between two deceivers.

Jacob's journey to Haran and back again has been long and painful. Now, on the brink of returning home to the land God promised him, Jacob has finally learned that his God is faithful. As he prepared for the next challenge of his journey—confronting the brother he had wronged—Jacob could be confident in God's continuing presence and care.

# THROUGHOUT THE BIBLE

Once the two deceiving men finally reached a settlement, they set up a pile stones at Mizpah to commemorate their agreement. Their actions reflect a common behavior in biblical times, as people often used stones to help them remember significant events. Earlier, Jacob had set up a stone after his vision at Bethel (Gen 28:22); when he later returns to Bethel, he will set up another stone to mark the place God had spoken with him (Gen 35:14).

Stone memorials are particularly prevalent in the book of Joshua. During the time the Israelites were conquering the land of Canaan, they set up seven memorials. The first was constructed after they had miraculously crossed the Jordan River to enter the land of promise. The priests gathered stones from the Jordan River, heaping them together as a reminder of how God brought his people across the Jordan on dry land. When later generations asked about the stones, the Israelites were to tell them about this miraculous event (Josh 4:6-7).

> **Quick Bit:** The Israelites set up memorial stones for crossing the Jordan River in Joshua 4, but it is unclear exactly how many piles they made. Some scholars think they set up one heap *in* the river (Josh 4:9) and another at Gilgal, a town near Jericho (Josh 4:2-4; 8, 20). Others think the larger context of the book of Joshua indicates only one pile of stones.

Two more memorials commemorated God's victory over Israel's Canaanite enemies. The people put heaps of stones over the grave of the king of Ai (Josh 8:28-29) and over the cave where the bodies of the five defeated Amorite kings were buried (Josh 10:27). Joshua also marked one Israelite grave with stones—Achan's. When Achan stole treasure from fallen Jericho, he disobeyed God and caused Israel's defeat at Ai (Josh 7:4-15). His entire family was stoned and burned in the Valley of Achor, and the people put a great heap of stones over the place (Josh 7:24-26) to serve as a reminder of the cost of disobedience.

Another two memorials signified Israel's commitment to keep the law of Moses in the promised land. Shortly after arriving in Canaan, the Israelites gathered at Mount Ebal, where they built an altar with stones from the Jordan River (Deut 27:4–7). They rejoiced that God had brought them across the Jordan into their land. Then Joshua recorded a copy of the law on stones to remind the people of how they were to conduct themselves in the land (Josh 8:32–34). When the conquest was complete, Joshua set up a stone at Shechem to mark the place where the Israelites renewed their commitment to God's covenant (Josh 24:26–27).

A final stone memorial was constructed in Gilead after a misunderstanding between the tribes. Two and a half Israelite tribes settled on the east side of the Jordan River while the others settled on the west. The eastern tribes (Gad, Reuben, and half of Manasseh) built an altar to signify their unity with the western tribes (Josh 22:26–27). But the western tribes misunderstood, thinking the altar was for worshiping other gods, so they prepared to battle the eastern tribes (Josh 22:10–12). When the western tribes understood the altar's true purpose, they made peace, and the stone stood as testimony that the eastern tribes also worshiped Yahweh (Josh 22:34).

God brought Jacob's descendants into the land he promised to their forefather, Abraham. He wanted them to remember how he miraculously parted the Jordan River for them, how he conquered their enemies, and how they committed to obey him. When the people of Israel saw the stone memorials, they would remember that God had been and always would be faithful to his promises.

## BEYOND THE BIBLE

Ancient interpreters insisted that the biblical patriarchs and matriarchs reflect a morality fitting of their legacy as founders of the faith. Behavior viewed as unbecoming of a devout follower of God had to be explained and justified (see "Beyond the Bible" in Chapter 2). Rachel's theft of her father's household gods was particularly troubling on two accounts: Stealing was wrong, but idolatry was worse. Surely Rachel wasn't taking these idols in order to worship them, was she? To soften the impact of Rachel's deed, a Targum subtly substituted the word "took" for "stole" in the Aramaic version of Genesis 31:19.[5] When the Jewish historian Josephus retells this story, he clarifies that Jacob had taught Rachel about the evils of idol worship, and that she took the idols to have a potential bargaining chip with Laban.

> **Quick Bit:** The name "Targum" comes from the Aramaic word *trgm*, meaning "to explain or translate." The Targums are a series of Aramaic translations of the Hebrew Bible (the OT). *Targum Onqelos* contains explanatory expansions to the Pentateuch.

> But the reason why Rachel took the images of the gods, although Jacob had taught her to despise such worship of those gods, was this: That in case they were pursued, and taken by her father, she might have recourse to these images, in order to obtain his pardon.[6]

In Josephus' view, Rachel's act was strategic, not immoral. She knew the idols weren't for worship. She took them to have leverage over Laban.

Other interpreters, both Jewish and Christian, suggest that Rachel stole the idols out of a moral desire to combat idolatry in her father's household:

> Her purpose in this was on God's behalf; for she said: "Now we are going our way. Can we leave this old man in the midst of his idolatry?" That is why Scripture found it necessary to say, "And Rachel stole ... "[7]

According to this interpretation, rather than take the idols for worship, Rachel was removing them from Laban's house to prevent *him* from worshiping them. This tradition is similar to stories about Abraham's early life when he opposed the idolatry of his father's house and even destroyed the idols through arson (*Jubilees* 12:1–8, 12–14). Believing there must be some lesson to be learned through Rachel's actions, these interpreters exonerate her from the charges of theft and idol worship by attributing pious motivation to her act.

The biblical version of events is much more ambiguous, leaving many questions unanswered. In doing so, it grants Rachel her humanity. Real people make mistakes. They don't always act out of upright intentions. In the biblical account, we find a more human Rachel who is committed to an uncertain future with her husband, but hesitant to leave her old life behind.

## APPLICATION

Up to this point, the relationship between Jacob and God has been one-sided. Jacob sought wealth and safety for himself without asking for God's help, and God blessed Jacob's prosperity and protected him from Laban (Gen 31:9, 29). Despite Jacob's attempts to secure for himself what God had promised him (Gen 28:15), God remained faithful to his word by blessing and protecting the patriarch. God's faithfulness was not frustrated by Jacob's faithlessness.

Paul writes about God's ultimate act of faithfulness in the face of human infidelity in his letter to the Romans. In Romans 1:18–2:11, Paul demonstrates that all people have sinned against God by dishonoring him and testing his patience. As a result, Paul writes that everyone has fallen short of God's glory (Rom 3:23). However, God kept his promises to the Jews (Rom 3:1–8) and, ultimately, to humanity in general, in his greatest display of faithfulness—the death of Christ, which is *for us* (Rom 5:8). Yet Paul also reminds us that God proved his faithfulness to us while we were still sinners and "enemies" of God (Rom 3:8–10).

Together, the story of Jacob and Paul's words in Romans illustrate an important truth about God's character: His faithfulness is not contingent upon human faithfulness—whether Jacob's or ours. At this point, Jacob is just beginning to recognize God's hand in his prosperity. He will eventually acknowledge that God has been with him throughout his *entire* life (Gen 35:2–3), but only after being wounded by God (Gen 32:22–32). As believers, we should learn to trust God's character rather than acting out of self-interest. We should learn early on what it took Jacob many years to understand. For God has given believers a greater promise of his presence than Jacob ever had—the Holy Spirit, the Spirit of God himself (Rom 8:1–17).

# DISCUSSION

## A Closer Look

1. Have you ever questioned God during a long season of difficulty? In hindsight, what did that experience teach you about God's faithfulness to you?

_____

_____

_____

2. Jacob deserved his brother's wrath, but he did nothing to earn his uncle's meanness. What right and wrong responses can we learn from Jacob's interactions with Laban?

_____

_____

_____

## Throughout the Bible

1. What kinds of situations today prompt us to erect memorials? How are these similar to or different from the memorials described in the Bible?

_____

_____

_____

2. What visual reminders can you use to trigger memories of God's faithfulness to you?

_____

_____

_____

**Beyond the Bible**

1. Think about stories you've heard people tell about their past. Do they tend to emphasize the positive or give you a real glimpse into their doubts and motivations?

_____

_____

_____

2. Reflect on a time when you chose to give someone the benefit of the doubt.

_____

_____

_____

**Application**

1. During what times in your life do you find it difficult to trust God's faithfulness?

_____

_____

_____

2. What do you think caused Jacob to often act out of self-interest rather than trusting God? What prevents you from trusting him?

_____

_____

_____

## CHAPTER 6

# PLEADING FOR PROTECTION

*Read Genesis 32:1–33:20.*

## SETTING THE STAGE

**Theme.** In a world that emphasizes independence and empowerment, it's easy to become too self-reliant. We like to take matters into our own hands, to seize control of our lives. But this idea of complete control and independence is an illusion. When we relinquish control of our lives to God, allowing him to work through us, we find that our struggle for control was fruitless and unnecessary.

Jacob took self-reliance a step too far. In his adolescence, he manipulated and deceived others to get what he wanted. When his own misdeeds caused him to flee from home, he even tried to manipulate God by making vows that were conditional on God blessing him (Gen 28:20–22). Now, as a grown man with a large family and wealth to protect, Jacob faced a situation beyond his control: Esau, the brother who vowed to kill him (Gen 27:41–42), was approaching with 400 men. Desperate and afraid, Jacob humbly called out for God to protect him (Gen 32:9–11). He literally wrestled with God, refusing to give up until God blessed him. Jacob emerged from this confrontation broken and limping, but with the recognition that he owed his life to God's deliverance (Gen 32:30).

**Literary Context.** Jacob had finally escaped Laban's household. He spent 20 years of his life laboring for Laban instead of "a few days" as he originally intended (see Gen 27:44). During this time, God had blessed

Jacob, making him prosperous and wealthy (Gen 30:25-43) and giving him 11 sons and one daughter through his two wives and their servants (Gen 29:31-30:22). Now, Jacob was finally en route home to Canaan.

But in leaving Haran, Jacob was forced to confront the conflict with his brother, Esau, that he had avoided for 20 years. Jacob had fled after stealing his brother's blessing (Gen 27:6-29). Before that, Jacob had manipulated his brother into selling him his birthright (Gen 25:29-34). After being cheated twice by Jacob (Gen 27:36), Esau was enraged. He vowed to kill Jacob, but their mother, Rebekah, learned of his intent and intervened, sending Jacob away to her brother to find a wife (Gen 27:41-45).

Jacob's life in Haran is bracketed by divine encounters. On his way to Haran, Jacob dreamed of angels going up and down a ladder from earth to heaven (Gen 28:10-22). God himself addressed Jacob, directly repeating the promise he had made to Abraham and Isaac. Jacob responded to this event with surprise (Gen 28:16). Then, he made a vow to God that was conditional on God staying with him and providing for him (Gen 28:20-22).

Now, as Jacob waited in fear for Esau's arrival, he had a second encounter with God (Gen 32:22-32)—one that mirrored the first. Jacob's second divine encounter came shortly after he again asked God to protect him, this time from Esau (Gen 32:11). Alone and anxious on the banks of the Jabbok, Jacob encountered a mysterious "man" and "wrestled with him until the breaking of the dawn" (Gen 32:24). This time, Jacob refused to let go until the man blessed him (Gen 32:26).

**Historical & Cultural Background.** Genesis 32:22-32 describes Jacob's wrestling partner on the riverbank as simply a "man," but after the encounter, Jacob claimed that he had seen God face to face (Gen 32:30). The "man's" statement that Jacob had "struggled with God" also seems to indicate that Jacob's opponent was in fact God (see also Hos 12:3). With this encounter, Jacob joined the ranks of many individuals in the OT who experienced a theophany[1]—an appearance of God on earth.

God appeared throughout the OT to people in different forms. Sometimes a theophany occurred in a vision, as was the case with Abraham (Gen 15:1). Other times, it occurred in dream, as with Solomon (1 Kgs 3:5). Jacob's first encounter with God also took place in a dream. In the second,

God appeared in the form of a man—and not for the first time. When God appeared to Abraham in Genesis 18, Abraham saw three men (Gen 18:1-2).

Often, theophanies included storms or displays of the power of nature. God's presence, in the form of a pillar of cloud and a pillar of fire, led the Israelites after they left Egypt (Exod 13:21-22). He appeared to Moses and the Israelites on Mount Sinai with thunder, lightning, and clouds (Exod 19:16-19). And God answered Job from a whirlwind (Job 38:1). When Solomon dedicated the temple, God's presence filled the holy of holies in the form of a cloud (1 Kgs 8:10-11).

The amazing theophanies in Jacob's life should have helped him recognize God's presence and protection. However, in both events, Jacob seemed most concerned with looking out for himself. Although he acknowledged God's faithfulness to him (Gen 32:10), Jacob continued to try to manipulate the situation for his own preservation (Gen 32:13-21). The impending confrontation with Esau, the brother he had cheated, would help him recognize the role God has played in his life. As Waltke says in his commentary, "The runaway must now confront his past with his family and his future with God."[2]

## A CLOSER LOOK

Bags have been packed. Goodbyes have been said. Farewell tensions have been resolved. Jacob has finally escaped from Laban. As Jacob left in relief, he encountered angels for the second time in his life (compare the moment at Bethel in Gen 28:12). "This is God's camp!" he exclaimed, and he named the place Mahanaim, which means "two camps" (Gen 32:1-2). God's camp was moving alongside Jacob's camp—a visible reminder to Jacob that God was with him for what he faced ahead: Esau.

Esau lived in Seir, the hill country of Edom. Jacob could have avoided Esau and gone straight to Canaan, but perhaps he felt the need to resolve things with his brother. Dispatching two servants with a message for Esau, Jacob alerted his brother of his return and his wish to be on good terms. Jacob's language showed his fear: He called Esau "my lord" and himself "your servant" (Gen 32:4-5). Twenty years earlier, Jacob had overreached his position in the family and stolen his brother's birthright and blessing. Now he took no chances by hoping that his brother had forgiven him.

> **Quick Bit:** Jacob tried to curry favor with Esau by calling him "my lord" and referring to himself as "your servant." You can often assess characters' thoughts or motives by how they address or refer to other characters. For example, in Genesis 16, neither Abram nor Sarai refer to Hagar by name. She is "my/your servant," their property. Only the narrator and Yahweh call her by name.

Jacob's fear turned to terror when his servants reported that Esau was coming to meet him with an army of 400 men—more men than his grandfather, Abraham, had gone to battle with in Genesis 14 (318 men). Apparently nothing had changed for Esau. He still wanted to kill Jacob. Jacob could not believe he had come this far to die at the hands of the brother he had fled.

Panicked about what Esau might do to his family, Jacob divided his entourage into two camps to minimize his losses. Then he prayed to the God who told him to return to his family and country so that he could bless him in the land of promise. This is the first time we have heard Jacob pray since he made his vow at Bethel, and this time, he didn't bargain with God. He loathed being Laban's servant, but he willingly called himself Yahweh's servant (Gen 32:10). He humbly acknowledged the kindness that God had shown him since he left Canaan destitute, and he pleaded for God to protect him from Esau and keep his promise to make things go well for him (Gen 32:11–12).

Jacob spent the night preparing for the next day's meeting. He assembled a generous gift for his brother (a total of 550 animals). Then he staggered his servants with portions of the gift and sent them on ahead. Upon meeting Esau, each was to say the flocks and herds with him belong to "your servant, to Jacob" and is "a gift ... to my lord, Esau" (Gen 32:18). Jacob hoped to overwhelm Esau with his wealth (and power) and soften him with waves of gifts. "Perhaps he will show me favor," he hoped (Gen 32:20).

With his peace offering on its way, Jacob sent his entourage across the Jabbok River and spent a sleepless night alone—just the way he had left Canaan. But he wasn't really alone then, and he wouldn't be now.

God appeared to him at Bethel, and he appears to him again on this important night—though we do not know it is God until later in the story. What we do know is that suddenly, Jacob was wrestling with an unknown man. The text is silent about where this assailant came from and why he fought with Jacob. And the text is cryptic about this figure's identity. The narrator simply calls him "the man." It is only as Jacob realized his opponent's real identity that we also know it. The men wrestled through the night, but neither gained the advantage.

As the sun peeked over the horizon, the mysterious man touched Jacob's hip, and it promptly popped out of joint. Instead of collapsing to the ground, the crippled Jacob tightened his grip on his opponent. When the man demanded that Jacob let him go, Jacob refused: "Not until you bless me," he demanded. Jacob's throbbing hip, dislocated with just a touch, told him that his assailant was no mere man, and thus Jacob demanded that his opponent bless him. This is not something a mystery man would have the authority to do. Jacob's hip told him he was in the presence of God, and his demand for a blessing tells us that he knew it.

The "man's" blessing begins with a question: "What is your name?" The patriarch's response takes us back to the beginning of his story in Genesis 25:26, when Isaac and Rebekah named their second-born twin Jacob—because he came out clutching his brother's heel. Jacob spent his life trying to gain the advantage, often succeeding at others' expense.

The "man" blessed Jacob by changing his name from Jacob—the one who fought to get to the top—to Israel, meaning "God fights" (Gen 32:28). His new name called him to believe that God would go before him and fight for him. Before he met with Esau and then moved back into the land of promise, Jacob needed to hear this. The newly named "Israel" named the place Peniel ("the face of God") and limped away to meet his brother (Gen 32:30).

**Quick Bit:** Jacob asked the assailant for his name, but the man didn't give it. Jacob's request might reflect an ancient belief that knowing the name of a god or supernatural being enabled a person to use the name for magical purposes.

When Esau's army came into view, Jacob divided up his family. Although he may now have some confidence in God's ability to fight, he still feels that he may lose this battle if he engages it, so he plans to minimize his losses if things go badly. He may also be trying to protect at least half of his people if he dies, giving them time to flee. At the front of the line he put his servant-wives (Bilhah and Zilpah) and their children (Dan, Naphtali, Gad, Asher). Behind them were Leah and her children (Reuben, Simeon, Levi, Judah, Issachar, Zebulun), and he tucked Rachel and Joseph safely in the back (Gen 33:1–2). Jacob hurried on ahead and bowed to the ground seven times in submission before he reached his brother.

Esau's reaction must have stunned Jacob: He ran to meet him, embraced him, "fell on his neck" and kissed him (Gen 33:4). The brothers wept together, and Esau gushed over Jacob's family (Gen 33:5). Then he told Jacob he shouldn't have bothered with the gifts because he had plenty already. But Jacob insisted that Esau accept the *blessing* he offers. Jacob's word choice is not accidental: He signaled to his brother that he was trying to make up for stealing his blessing years earlier. When Esau accepted and did not offer a gift in return, we can utter a sigh of relief that the ancient score between the brothers has been settled.

Jacob had made things right with Esau, but he still didn't trust him. When Esau invited Jacob to travel with him back to Seir, Jacob declined, insisting that his group would only slow them down (Gen 33:12–14). He urged Esau to go on without him and assured him that they would be right behind him. Esau offered to loan Jacob some servants to make the trip easier, but Jacob politely insisted his party would be fine (Gen 33:15). Finally, he persuaded Esau to go home and not wait for him.

But Jacob had no intention of following his brother to Seir. Esau departed to the south, and Jacob turned around and headed north to Succoth, near the Jordan River (Gen 33:17). He settled in Succoth for a time before finally returning to Canaan. He may have wanted to pasture his flocks and herds in the fertile valley there until he could recoup what he had given to Esau.[3]

From Succoth, Jacob crossed the Jordan and camped near Shechem, where he eventually bought a piece of land. Then Jacob built an altar to God, the God of Israel (*El-Elohe-Israel*), who brought him safely back from his exile in Haran. Twenty years after Jacob first met God and offered him a conditional vow, Jacob was convinced that his God could be trusted. He was now ready to live up to his new name of Israel.

## THROUGHOUT THE BIBLE

Jacob's wrestling match with the unnamed man at Peniel was a defining moment in his life. His opponent gave him a new name to reflect this monumental moment—"Your name shall no longer be called Jacob, but Israel, for you have struggled with God and with men and have prevailed" (Gen 32:28). Jacob's original name, which means "he supplants" (Gen 25:26), had defined him from birth to his encounter with God at Peniel. Jacob's new name, which means "God fights," redefined the patriarch, challenging him to trust his God as he returned to the land of Canaan.

Name changes are a frequent and significant feature of the OT. One of the first characters in the Bible to receive a new name is Abram. When God made a covenant with Abram, he gave to Abram a new name—"Abraham," meaning "father of many nations" (Gen 17:5). Abraham's new name is directly related to his role as the originator of a family through whom God will bless the whole world (Gen 15:6–8). Abraham's wife, Sarai, also receives a new name (Gen 17:15). In this case, what is significant is not the meaning of the given name (Sarah), which is almost identical to the original name, but that God gave her a new name that suited her new role as the mother of Abraham's offspring.

Later in the Genesis narrative, Pharaoh gives Joseph the Egyptian name Zaphenath-paneah to reflect his ability to interpret dreams (Gen 41:45). In many countries it was customary to give captives new names as a sign of their assimilation into their new culture. This practice is reflected in the story of Daniel and his fellow Hebrews, each of whom received a Babylonian name from the king (Dan 1:6–7). One of the most striking instances of renaming in the OT is found in Hosea. In Hosea 1, God symbolically names Hosea's children, the last of whom is given the name "*Lo-ammi*" (Hos 1:9), which means "not my people," which directly refutes the covenant formula in Exodus 6:7.

There are also significant name changes in the NT. Jesus' renaming of the disciples—especially Peter—plays a key role in the narrative of the gospels. Jesus renames Simon "Peter," which means "rock" (Mark 3:16). In a later scene in the Gospels, Jesus declares, "you are Peter, and on this rock I will build my church" (Matt 16:18). Jesus not only changes Peter's name but anticipates his role in the growth of the Church. In the book of Acts, the Pharisee Saul decided to go by the name Paul as he embarked on his missionary journeys. Paul's decision to use his Roman name was probably motivated by his role as a missionary primarily to Gentiles. In the book of Revelation, Christ promises to give believers a white stone with a "new name," which likely refers to the final blessing when Christ returns, anticipated in Isaiah 62:2.

Throughout the Bible, name changes occur for two reasons. Sometimes the name change is based on the meaning of the new name. More often, though, an individual receives a new name that is appropriate for a new role or task they have been given. Both motivations seem to be true in the case of Jacob. Instead of bearing a name that reflected his deceptive past, he was given the name to match his role as the eponymous head of a people for whom God will fight.

## BEYOND THE BIBLE

One of the most curious events of Jacob's life was his physical encounter with some sort of supernatural being in Genesis 32:22–32. In the biblical account, this being is identified only as a "man," but Jacob later understood him to have been God himself (Gen 32:30). This ambiguity was difficult for ancient interpreters to accept. How could Jacob have wrestled all night with the Almighty God and "prevailed" (Gen 32:28)? Even the Bible itself later identifies the "man" as both God and an angel (Hos 12:3–4).

> **Quick Bit:** Origen was an early church father based in Alexandria and then Caesarea in the early third century AD (d. AD 253). He was widely respected as a scholar well-versed in Greek literature, philosophy, and biblical interpretation, but he experienced tension with church leaders over some of his teachings that were viewed as unorthodox. His theology is heavily influenced by his wide learning in

Greek philosophy, but his interpretation was based on very careful study of the grammatical nuances of the Greek text of Scripture.

One of the more innovative solutions to this question focuses on the meaning of "struggled with God" in Genesis 32:28. Perhaps the meaning was not that Jacob wrestled with God as his adversary, but with God as his ally. The church father Origen eloquently explained this interpretation:

> [A] man perhaps would never be able of himself to vanquish an op-posing power, unless he had the benefit of divine assistance. Hence, also, the angel is said to have wrestled with Jacob. Here, however, I understand the writer to mean, that it was not the same thing for the angel to have wrestled *with* Jacob, and to have wrestled *against* him; but the angel that wrestles with him is he who was present with him in order to secure his safety, who, after knowing also his moral progress, gave him in addition the name of Israel, i.e., he is with him in the struggle, and assists him in the contest; seeing *there was undoubtedly another angel against whom he contended*, and against whom he had to carry on a contest. Finally, Paul has not said that we wrestle with princes, or with powers, but against prin-cipalities and powers. And hence, although Jacob wrestled, it was unquestionably against some one of those powers which, Paul de-clares, resist and contend with the human race, and especially with the saints. And therefore at last the Scripture says of him that "he wrestled with the angel, and had power with God," so that *the strug-gle is supported by help of the angel*, but the prize of success conducts the conqueror to God [emphasis added].[4]

For Origen, the solution was simple: Jacob was not wrestling God, but the spiritual forces of evil (Eph 6:12). Spiritual warfare requires divine as-sistance. Jacob could not battle these forces alone, so God himself sent help in the form of an angel to assist him in the struggle. Whether the an-gel was fighting with or against Jacob, once again Jacob had encountered God's presence when he needed it most.

# APPLICATION

Like Jacob, most of us like to be in control of our lives. When we succeed, we assume it's because we worked hard. Sometimes we even manipulate people and situations to guarantee our success. But many of us also live with the fear that everything we've worked for will come crashing down. The carefully constructed lives we maintain are just one phone call, meeting, or accident away from disaster. We feel like we are balancing on a tightrope between great success and catastrophe—and the outcome is in our hands.

The night that Jacob prepared to meet his brother, he was a self-made man haunted by the fear that he would lose everything. He cried out to God for protection, but then he fought with all his strength against God in the flesh. Jacob's night-long struggle left him limping, but changed—at least for the time. He would continue to struggle with fear and faith when he reached Canaan. And God continued to protect and bless him anyway.

It is difficult to trust God to take care of us when we feel helpless. We struggle to regain control, and sometimes we even fight against God. But God is on our side, and he promises to be with us no matter what we face (Psa 118:6; Heb 13:5). He has the control that we wrestle to get, and we only hurt ourselves and slow our spiritual growth when we don't acknowledge that he is our life, strength, and refuge.

## DISCUSSION

**A Closer Look**

1. How has God reassured you when you have feared something?

_____

_____

_____

2. Have you ever returned to old fears even after God reassured you? What can you learn about fear from the story of Jacob?

_____

_____

_____

**Throughout the Bible**

1. Can you think of other people in the Bible who were given a new name? How was their new name fitting for their new identity?

_____

_____

_____

2. For many of these biblical figures, receiving a new name meant leaving behind part of their past. What things do you leave behind as you accept your new identity in Christ?

_____

_____

_____

## Beyond the Bible

1. Reflect on a time when you felt God's comfort or reassurance in an unexpected way.

_____

_____

_____

2. Have you ever found yourself engaged in spiritual warfare? How did you deal with the circumstances?

_____

_____

_____

## Application

1. In what areas of your life do you most fear losing control? How has God challenged your belief that you even have control in those areas?

_____

_____

_____

2. Reflect on a time when you knew you were helpless and God came through for you. How can you use this experience to help you trust him in the future?

_____

_____

_____

## CHAPTER 7

# A FAILED FATHER

*Read Genesis 34:1-31.*

## SETTING THE STAGE

**Theme.** How we respond to tragedy reveals our true character. When we allow God to shape us, we respond in faith—seeking him for assistance and guidance through the storm. When we follow our own impulses and instincts, we may react to tragedy with violent emotion and impulsive action. The biblical picture of a righteous person is one who is in regular communion with God. For the most part, Abraham, Moses, and Daniel all weathered difficulty in their lives by seeking God first. They experienced struggles when they did not.

In Genesis 34, Jacob and his family confronted the terrible news that Dinah, Jacob's only daughter, had been raped by a local prince. Her reputation had been tarnished, and the whole family faced dishonor and shame. The family now faced the difficult choice of how to respond to this event. If we were expecting Jacob to leap up and offer a righteous solution, we're sorely disappointed. Jacob's response was inaction. He didn't appeal to God's guidance, but he didn't respond with impulsive action either. He simply waited for his sons to return home. Because of Jacob's inaction and failure to seek God first, his vengeful sons took matters into their own hands, committing a wholesale massacre of the people of Shechem.

**Literary Context.** Having finally returned to the promised land, Jacob bought a piece of property from the sons of Hamor, prince of nearby Shechem (Gen 33:18-19). He built an altar there and called it El-Elohe-Israel, "God is the God of Israel" (Gen 33:20). Israel was the patriarch's new name, which he received after wrestling with God all night (Gen 32:28). As Israel settled back in the land of Canaan, he professed that God was *his* God, the God of Israel.

Yet in the troubling events concerning his daughter at Shechem (Gen 34), Jacob never turned to his God for help. Instead, he demonstrated lack of faith in God's promises and lack of concern for the descendants God had given him. The text clues the reader in to Jacob's shortcomings in at least two ways.

The first clue is the place, Shechem. Genesis mentions Shechem only once before this account. When Abram arrived in Canaan after his journey from Haran, he stopped first at Shechem (Gen 12:6). Like Jacob, Abram built an altar there to Yahweh, who promised to give "this land" to Abram's descendants (Gen 12:7). Jacob was Abram's descendant, the recipient of the promises Yahweh made to his forefather. Yet when he arrived at Shechem, Jacob bought a portion of the property that God had already promised to *give* him. Furthermore, Jacob remained silent in Genesis 34 as Hamor and his son made a deal to help the Israelites acquire surrounding property. The heir of God's covenant with Abraham appears to have doubted that God would give him the land.

The second clue begins in Genesis 34:1, when Dinah went out to see "the women of the land" (Gen 34:1). Like the name Shechem, the expression "women of the land" appears only once in Genesis before Genesis 34. Jacob's mother, Rebekah, despaired that her favored son might marry one of the "women of the land" (Gen 27:46), so Isaac sent him to find a wife among her family in Haran. Abraham had shown similar concern for Isaac's marriage and had also sent his servant to Haran (Gen 24). However, Jacob allowed his daughter to intermingle with these women and then stood by silently while his sons negotiated a deal with Hamor so that their families could intermarry. (See "Setting the Stage" in Chapters 1 and 3).

During his encounter with his brother in Genesis 32–33, Jacob recognized his own powerlessness and need for God's protecting power. God met him in his fear and changed his name from Jacob to a divine promise of protection (Israel means "God will fight," Gen 32:28). But in the next chapter, the new Israel struggled again with fear and weakness. Furthermore, he let hatred divide him from his sons, just as it had separated him from his own brother (Gen 27:41–45). The family tension evident in the Shechem event will only increase, coming to light again in Joseph's story.

**Historical & Cultural Background.** The prince of Shechem was determined to make Dinah his wife. As contemptible as his actions were toward Dinah, they reflect the cultural customs of his time. In the ancient world, marriages were arranged, and children typically had little say in the decision. Parents usually arranged marriages within their kinship group (see "Setting the Stage" in Chapters 1 and 3) or for political alliances.

One way children who wanted to marry someone else could escape such arrangements was to engage in illicit sex. If a girl was no longer a virgin—whether by rape or consensual sex[1]—her parents would have great difficulty making a good marriage for her. Thus, she would be married to the man who took her virginity. The would-be groom usually paid a premium bride price in return for the family's trouble and shame.[2]

Ancient Near Eastern law and later biblical law addressed such situations. Exodus 22:16–17 required the guilty man to marry the woman since her father would be unable to marry her to anyone else (see also Deut 22:28–29). This law guaranteed that she would have a husband, the primary means of survival for a woman in ancient society. In addition, a Sumerian law prescribed what should happen when a young woman was raped after leaving her parents' home without permission, and other ancient laws stipulated that a rapist must pay an especially high bride price.[3]

Genesis 34 does not explain Dinah's role in the events. The word translated "rape" implies that the man took initiative, but it can also apply to situations in which the girl shared the accountability (Deut 22:23–24). But whether Dinah was raped or consented to the act with Shechem is irrelevant to the story. The incident demeaned Dinah, who didn't have the "right of consent" in her ancient culture. Furthermore, the event shamed Dinah's family—especially so if she was complicit, since it would show a great lack of respect in her culture.[4] While Jacob failed to take action, Dinah's brothers accused Shechem of treating their sister like a prostitute because he intended to use her *and then* pay (Gen 34:31).

## A CLOSER LOOK

The trouble between Jacob's family and the Shechemites starts in Genesis 34:1, where we meet Dinah, "the daughter of Leah, whom she had borne to Jacob." Jacob never loved Leah, nor was he impressed with the sons she bore (Gen 30:32–34, 19–20). He was even less impressed with his daughter. In Genesis 34, Dinah went "out to see the women of the land" (Gen 34:1)—an unusual outing, in the culture, for an unchaperoned girl of marriageable age.[5] The narrator never indicts Dinah for the horrors that happened to her. Instead, the responsibility falls to her father, who failed to care for her before the rape and after.

Dinah encountered Shechem, whose father was chief over the city of Shechem and 1,000 square miles of rural territory in the hill country.[6] The chief's son "saw her ... took her ... lay with her ... and raped her" (Gen 34:2). Shechem's appalling actions against Jacob's daughter disgraced her and dishonored her entire family.

Then the story takes an unexpected turn: We are told that Shechem loved Dinah, spoke tenderly to her, and wanted to marry her properly (compare to Amnon, who hated Tamar after he raped her; 2 Sam 13:15–17). We don't learn until later that Dinah stayed in Shechem's house after the rape (Gen 34:17; 26), and we never learn whether she stayed by force or choice. Her brothers assumed the best of her and the worst of Shechem: She was held against her will.

Shechem's coarse demand of his father to "get this girl for me as a wife" betrayed him. Whatever his charms *might* have been, Shechem knew how to get his way, and he clearly viewed Dinah as property to be had. This trait will reappear when he and his father persuade the men of Shechem to yield to the demands of Dinah's brothers.

Word reached Jacob that Shechem had defiled his daughter, Dinah. We expect an outraged father to rush to his daughter's rescue and defend the honor of his family against the Canaanite brute. But Jacob kept silent (Gen 34:5; compare to David, who was "very angry" when Amnon raped his daughter; 2 Sam 13:21). Jacob's sons were a different story. When they heard the news, they stormed in from the field, ready to avenge their sister. These different reactions show a blatant contrast between Jacob and his sons: Jacob heard the news and was silent, waiting for his sons to return. The brothers heard the news and raced in from the field in a fury.

Before the brothers made it back to camp, Hamor swept in to speak with Jacob on behalf of his infatuated son. But he hadn't finished his proposal when Jacob's sons charged in (Gen 34:6-7). Hamor continued with his offer to marry his son to Jacob's daughter (Gen 34:8). But he had more in mind than just joining the families of Jacob and Hamor. He spoke on behalf of his entire territory: "Make marriages with us; give your daughters to us, and take our daughters to yourselves" (Gen 34:9). If the patriarch's people would intermarry with the people of the land, Hamor promised, "The land shall be open to you; live and trade in it, and get property in it" (Gen 34:10 NRSV).

Shechem went further, offering a name-your-price gift and bride price for Dinah (Gen 34:11-12). Neither man mentioned the violation of Dinah or the shame it brought on her family. Appealing instead to greed, Hamor and Shechem offered Jacob and his sons what looks like a bribe to brush over the offense.

> **Quick Bit:** Shechem offered to pay whatever bride price and additional gift Jacob's family asked of him. Usually bride prices were fixed by custom, so his extravagant "blank check" offer with an additional gift indicates that he recognized the need to atone for his unseemly behavior toward Dinah.

But neither Shechem's love nor the offer of money moved Dinah's brothers. The narrator clues us in that they were answering deceitfully when they responded to the extravagant offer. They refused the offer because the Shechemites were uncircumcised, outsiders to the Abrahamic covenant. However, if every male in Shechem were to get circumcised, the family of Jacob would intermarry with them and "become one people" (Gen 34:16 NRSV).

Hamor and Shechem agreed to the terms and then hurried back to town to persuade all the Shechemite men to undergo circumcision. The narrator prepares us for their success by telling us that Shechem was the "most honored of all his family" (Gen 34:19 NRSV). When he spoke alongside their leader, Hamor, the people would listen. In their pitch, father and son extolled the peacefulness of Jacob's family (Gen 34:21) and the potential benefits of intermarriage with them: "Will not their livestock, their property, and all their animals be ours?" (Gen 34:23 NRSV). Without any mention of Dinah, the men highlighted the economic advantage of intermarriage for the city and convinced the men that circumcision was a prudent choice for all of them. In the process, they hint at their intention to further take advantage of Jacob's tribe.

> **Quick Bit:** Hamor described the proposed alliance between the Shechemites and the Israelites twice: first to Jacob's sons and then to the men of Shechem. But he sold each group on a different arrangement, demonstrating that he, too, was deceitful. When we carefully listen to a character's speech, we can learn about their motives and character.

Three days later, when the men of Shechem were still healing from their circumcisions and thus defenseless, two of Jacob's sons exacted their revenge. Simeon and Levi slaughtered the men of the city and whisked Dinah away. Then the rest of the brothers plundered the city (Gen 34:25–29).

Jacob, silent in the text until now, finally spoke. But he did not decry the senseless slaughter, the abuse of the covenantal rite of circumcision, the opportunistic greed, or the deception that lay behind the brothers' heinous behavior. Instead, he rebuked only Simeon and Levi because their action made him "odious to the inhabitants of the land" (Gen 34:30 NRSV) and thus potentially endangered his life. Simeon and Levi may have had honorable motives, but they carried out disproportionate justice. Years later, when Jacob dies, he "blesses" these two sons with something more like a curse because of their actions at Shechem (Gen 49:5–7).

The appalling account ends with a question asked by the avenging brothers: "Should our sister be treated like a whore?" (Gen 34:31 NRSV). The answer hangs in the air and indicts Jacob for his passivity. His failure to protect his daughter, defend her honor, and then rein in his sons results in atrocity. Furthermore, Jacob said nothing in response to larger issues of the covenant that lay behind the proposed alliance between the Shechemites and the Israelites. Of great importance to both Abraham and Isaac was the marriage of their sons to women from their own kindred, yet Jacob did not protest Hamor's proposal for tribal intermarriage, which risked the entire covenant promise.

Furthermore, Jacob had returned to the land God promised him, yet he allowed his sons to negotiate a deal in which they could acquire property. The property was his by promise from God, but instead he viewed it as something to be bargained for, just like he has bargained for nearly everything else in his life. His passivity is, at best, careless indifference; at worst, it is a lack of faith that God would keep his promises to give Jacob the land and to multiply his descendants. His failure to act in faith on behalf of his family had disastrous effects.

# THROUGHOUT THE BIBLE

The tragic events of Genesis 34 do not feature prominently in the rest of the Bible. Later in Genesis, however, Simeon and Levi's actions against the sons of Shechem resurface as Jacob blesses his 12 sons prior to his death. Throughout Genesis 49, Jacob blesses each of his sons individually by pronouncing their share in his inheritance. However, he addresses Simeon and Levi together:

> Simeon and Levi are brothers; weapons of violence are their swords. Let me not come into their council. Let not my person be joined to their company. For in their anger they killed men, and at their pleasure they hamstrung cattle. Cursed be their anger, for it is fierce, and their wrath, for it is cruel. I will divide them in Jacob, and I will scatter them in Israel (Gen 49:5-7).

Instead of blessing and giving a portion of his inheritance to Simeon and Levi, Jacob effectively curses them by condemning their violence and angry behavior at Shechem. He also deprives them of their rightful share of his inheritance by dividing their portion among the other tribes (Gen 49:7).

Jacob's censure of Simeon and Levi is later fulfilled in the Pentateuch as the tribes of Israel receive their allotment of land, but it is fulfilled in an unexpected way. We learn in Joshua 19:1-9 that rather than inheriting its own territory of land, the tribe of Simeon was folded into the tribe of

Judah. The tribe of Levi was also made dependent upon the other tribes of Israel, but rather than residing within the land of another single tribe, the Levites were allotted 48 cities among the other tribes (Num 18:21–24; 35:1–8; Josh 21:1–45). The tribe of Levi was additionally given priestly responsibilities among the people of Israel and Yahweh himself as their inheritance (Deut 10:9).

The vengeful actions of Simeon and Levi in Genesis 34, as well as Jacob's cursing of their violence, altered the fate of their descendants in the biblical narrative. Although the Levites redeemed their tribe to a certain degree when they responded to Moses' call for faithful Israelites following the golden calf incident (Exod 32:25–29), their actions were once again characterized by violence.

## BEYOND THE BIBLE

The Shechem story has always troubled interpreters because the narrator does not seem to condemn Jacob's sons for the atrocities committed against the Shechemites. Since the narrator does not censure the actions of Simeon and Levi, perhaps their extreme actions were warranted— or even sanctioned by God. The line of reasoning continues to the conclusion that the entire city of Shechem may have been complicit in the rape of Dinah, or perhaps that the Dinah incident was just the last in a long history of violence against the defenseless. If so, the mass slaughter by Simeon and Levi was punishment decreed by God.

> **Quick Bit:** Judith is an apocryphal or deuterocanonical book of the Bible. It was written during the Second Temple period and is a dramatic story of deception. The deuterocanonical books can help us understand the culture and history of Judaism.

The deuterocanonical book of Judith reflects this understanding of Genesis 34. Judith was a beautiful Jewish widow living in the seventh century BC, when Israel was invaded by the Assyrians. Frustrated that her countrymen didn't trust God to deliver them from their enemies, Judith made a daring attempt to exact justice from the foreign conquerors. She dressed to kill—literally—and gave herself into the custody of the Assyrians under the ruse of offering them insider information.

Mesmerized by her beauty and flattery, the Assyrian general Holofernes made Judith his guest and then waited for the right moment to seduce her. She, however, had been waiting for the right moment to kill him, which she did one night when he was "dead drunk" (Judith 13:2). Judith decapitated the general and then smuggled his head back to her fearful countrymen. The leaderless Assyrians withdrew, and Israel was saved.

Before Judith had left Israel for her covert attack on the Assyrians, she cried out to God and appealed to the story of the Shechemites:

> O Lord God of my ancestor Simeon, to whom you gave a sword to take revenge on those strangers who had torn off a virgin's clothing to defile her, and exposed her thighs to put her to shame, and polluted her womb to disgrace her; for you said, "It shall not be done"—yet they did it; So you gave up their rulers to be killed, and their bed, which was ashamed of the deceit they had practiced, was stained with blood, and you struck down slaves along with princes, and princes on their thrones. You gave up their wives for booty and their daughters to captivity, and all their booty to be divided among your beloved children who burned with zeal for you and abhorred the pollution of their blood and called on you for help. O God, my God, hear me also, a widow (Judith 9:2–4 NRSV).

Just as Simeon had avenged the helpless Dinah, so the defenseless widow Judith would avenge the besieged Israelites. By Simeon's sword, God had struck down the depraved Shechemites, so Judith implored God to use her to do the same to the vile Assyrians.

Interpreters often struggle when biblical characters do horrible things and God does not respond in the way we think he should. We search for explanations when our sense of morality or justice is violated. However, the Bible does not always answer our questions about specific situations. Instead, it invites us into the story and lets us wrestle with the questions it creates.

## APPLICATION

The catchphrase "two steps forward, one step back" aptly describes Jacob's spiritual growth. In fact, his progress often looks more like "one step forward, two steps back." Jacob's encounter with God at Peniel (Gen 32) and his reconciliation with Esau (Gen 33) were high points in his spiritual journey. What happened at Shechem certainly represents one of his lowest points (Gen 34).

Spiritual growth can be painful and arduous. Our failures and besetting sins can sideline us, making us feel like we have made no progress. Jacob's life with God should encourage us that God can work through even our failures. God patiently helps us along, one little step at a time.

When we reflect upon how God has worked in our lives—through either journaling, praying, or some other reflective action—we are able to see how he uses both our successes and failures. We learn how he accomplishes his purposes, even (and often) in dire circumstances. We can also see how he thinks and feels about unjust circumstances and seek his guidance in each decision.

# DISCUSSION

## A Closer Look

1. Why do you think Jacob does nothing in this chapter except complain that his life might be in danger?

_____

_____

_____

2. How does this story reflect earlier events in Jacob's life?

_____

_____

_____

## Throughout the Bible

1. Simeon and Levi were not the only people in the Bible to respond to a situation with violence. Who else in the biblical narrative can you think of who resorted to violence to resolve a problem?

_____

_____

_____

2. The narrative of Genesis often uses negative examples to teach us about God and faith. What can you learn from the actions of Simeon and Levi in this story?

_____

_____

_____

**Beyond the Bible**

1. What other characters or stories in the Bible leave us with unanswered questions about morality or justice? How have you heard these situations explained?

_____

_____

_____

2. Does God ever exact his justice through people? If so, how does he do it? If not, how does he carry out justice?

_____

_____

_____

**Application**

1. Do you keep a journal as part of your devotional life? If so, how has this practice helped you?

_____

_____

_____

2. Have you ever had a "mountaintop" spiritual experience that was followed by a deep spiritual valley? How can the story of Jacob encourage you when that happens?

_____

_____

_____

## CHAPTER 8

# RENAMED AND RENEWED

*Read Genesis 35:1–29.*

## SETTING THE STAGE

**Theme.** Everyone's faith story is different. For some of us, the turn from death in sin to new life in Christ was swift and abrupt. Others continue to wrestle with uncertainty and doubt for years as God works in their lives to draw them closer to a relationship with him. Many of us struggle our whole lives to balance our feelings of uncertainty and inadequacy with the certainty and sufficiency of faith in Christ.

Jacob's commitment to God seems to have been on again, off again. He struggled to work through fears and doubts until the assurance of faith finally overcame his hesitation and became the guiding principle of his life. Throughout Jacob's journey, he struggled to commit himself fully to God—qualifying his commitment with conditions that God must meet to prove his power (Gen 28). As Jacob prepared to return to Bethel, he finally acknowledged the sovereignty of God over his life and his household: The God of Abraham and Isaac became the God of Jacob (Gen 35:3).

**Literary Context.** Jacob's sons had just annihilated Shechem, killing their men and plundering the city. Retaliation from neighboring nations seemed imminent. But instead of being attacked for the actions of his sons, Jacob received direct orders from God: "Arise, Go up to Bethel and dwell there, and make an altar to the God who appeared to you when you fled from before Esau your brother" (Gen 35:1). His instructions allude back to Genesis 28:10-22, when God first appeared to Jacob in a dream and spoke to him, repeating the covenant promise he had made to Abraham and Isaac (Gen 28:13-14). God had also promised Jacob that he would be with him and bring him back to the land he was in (Gen 28:15).

At the time, Jacob was fleeing from his brother, who wanted to kill him. Jacob's response to God's words of promise betrayed his reluctance. He made a vow that was contingent on God doing what he had just promised to do: If God would protect him, provide for him, and return him home, then Jacob would call Yahweh *his* God (Gen 28:20-21).

Now Jacob had reconciled with his brother and returned to Canaan a wealthy man with a large family. God had fulfilled all of Jacob's conditions: He had protected him, provided for him, and brought him home to Canaan. By calling Jacob to go back to Bethel and build an altar, God was reminding Jacob that it was time to fulfill *his* side of the vow (Gen 35:1; see 28:22).[1] Jacob responded with complete obedience. First, he eradicated any foreign gods from his household and acknowledged that God had been with him wherever he went (Gen 35:2-3). Then he built an altar and worshiped his God, the God of his fathers.

**Historical & Cultural Background.** Jacob's first response after receiving God's orders to return to Bethel was to clear his household of any idols. It may surprise us that there were idols in his family to begin with, but idols were a common part of life in the ancient Near East. The foreign gods Jacob referred to were most likely household gods, or *teraphim*, like those Rachel stole from Laban (Gen 31:19). These *teraphim* were figurines made to represent deities. They are distinguished from other idols that would be set up in temples or shrines in that they were smaller and more portable.

Household gods may have been used as an attempted means to bring good fortune and protection upon a household or family.[2] Ancients also probably used them for divination—a means of gaining information or determining future actions (see Ezek 21:21). Additionally, household gods may have been related to inheritance rights. One Mesopotamian legal document seems to associate a man's estate with his household gods.[3]

Whatever the precise function of the household gods, they were likely valuable. Jacob's decision to discard them shows that he was serious about fulfilling his vow. However weak his commitment to God had been in the past, now Jacob is ready to commit. Cleansing his camp of other gods, Jacob earnestly acknowledges that God has been with him all this time and would continue to protect him (Gen 35:3–5).

# A CLOSER LOOK

With the blood of an entire city on his hands and plunder from the massacre still in his camp, Jacob looked fearfully toward the surrounding nations, expecting an attack at any time. His family was guilty of great atrocity, and Jacob was aware of it. But no attack came. Instead, Jacob received instructions from God to travel to Bethel and build an altar. Years earlier, Jacob had spent the night in Bethel as he fled from the brother he had wronged (Gen 35:1). God had appeared to him in a dream, and Jacob had vowed to accept God as his God on the condition that God protect him and provide for him (Gen 28:20–22). God had kept his promise, and now Jacob must keep his vow.

Jacob alerted his household that they were leaving Shechem. But first, the patriarch gathered all the idols in the camp and buried them under a tree (Gen 35:2, 4). The text does not tell us where these "foreign gods" came from, but some of them were probably Laban's household gods, which Rachel had stolen on the flight from Haran (Gen 31:19). Jacob's company also included the captives and plunder from the Shechem raid, which likely included idols (Gen 34:29; 35:2). As he buried these other gods deep in the ground, Jacob officially renounced any other god in fulfillment of his vow to make Yahweh his God in return for bringing him safely back to the land (Gen 28:20–21).

Jacob commanded his entourage to purify themselves and change their clothes in preparation for the meeting at Bethel. The text doesn't tell us why the camp was defiled, but the bloodshed and contact with corpses at Shechem may have been the cause (Gen 34; compare Num 31:19). Then Jacob told his household that he would build an altar to the God who answered him in his distress (Gen 35:3). He was likely referring to his trouble with Esau, but Jacob had endured a lot of difficulty in his life. God had been with him at every step (Gen 35:3), even when Jacob was completely undeserving.

By moving his camp to Bethel, Jacob left his household vulnerable to attack. But his fear of attack proved unfounded (Gen 34:30). Instead, the surrounding cities had the fear of God in them; no one dared retaliate against the Israelites (Gen 35:5).

Jacob arrived safely at Bethel and erected an altar, as God commanded. Then he renamed the sacred place El-Bethel, "the God of Bethel" (literally, "the God of the house of God"). The narrator explains Jacob's reason for the new name: "God had appeared to him when he fled before his brother" (Gen 35:7). When Jacob first named the place Bethel ("house of God"), he simply acknowledged that the place was sacred because God had been there (Gen 28:17). Now God has taken care of Jacob, and the place becomes much less significant than the God who met him there.[4]

God appeared to Jacob again, blessed him, and reiterated Jacob's name change from Jacob to Israel (Gen 35:9-10; compare Gen 32:28). This time, we do not receive an explanation for the name change; the narrator assumes we remember the previous story (Gen 35:9-10). Then God affirmed to Jacob the same covenant he made with Abraham. He had promised Abraham land, a great nation, and even nations of descendants (Gen 12:1-3; 17:1-8), and Jacob is the heir of that promise. Like he did on his first trip to Bethel, Jacob set up a pillar of stone to commemorate the place and poured oil over it. But this time, he also made a drink offering on the pillar (Gen 35:14).

> **Quick Bit:** In the middle of Jacob's encounter with God at Bethel, the narrator tells us that Deborah, Rebekah's nurse, died and was buried there (Gen 35:8). This woman barely appears in Genesis 24:59, and the reason for her presence here is unclear. Jewish tradition says Rebekah sent Deborah to bring Jacob back from Haran, in fulfillment of her promise to do so (Gen 27:45), but she would have been 130 at the time and an unlikely candidate for the task.[5]

Jacob's family then continued their journey, heading south toward Ephrath. En route, Rachel went into hard labor and gave birth to her second son. Her prayer at the birth and naming of her first son, Joseph ("May the Lord add to me another son"; Gen 30:24 ESV), is answered. However, after Rachel named the new baby Ben-oni ("son of my sorrow"; Gen 35:17-19), she tragically died. Jacob renamed his newest son Benjamin instead ("son of my right hand"; Gen 35:18), then buried his beloved Rachel (Gen 35:19-20). After the burial, the narrator calls Jacob by his new name, Israel: "Israel journeyed on and pitched his tent beyond the tower of Eder" (Gen 35:21). He has finally transitioned in faith.

While the family camped near the tower of Eder, Israel experienced further hardship from his sons: Reuben, his firstborn, slept with his father's servant-wife, Bilhah, the mother of Dan and Naphtali. The barren Rachel had given Bilhah to Jacob so that she could bear sons for him through her servant (Gen 30:3-8). Now that Rachel was dead, Reuben likely feared that Bilhah would become Jacob's favorite wife instead of his own mother, Leah. By violating her, Reuben prevented this from happening and confined Bilhah to "living widowhood"[6] (compare Absalom's actions with David's concubines in 2 Sam 16:22 and David's response in 2 Sam 20:3). But Reuben's actions go further than simply securing his mother's position. By sleeping with Jacob's concubine, Reuben attempted to seize his father's power (compare Adonijah's request for David's concubine, Abishag in 1 Kgs 2:13-25; he was condemned for treason).

The narrator leaves a gap where we expect to find Jacob's response to Reuben's insolence. He tells us only that "Israel heard about it" (Gen 35:22), leaving us to wonder whether Jacob was indifferent (as he was in Dinah's situation; Gen 34:5) or impotent before his eldest son. We only learn much later that Jacob was outraged. At the end of Genesis, when Jacob blessed his sons, his "blessing" of Reuben became a curse (Gen 49:3-4). By his actions, Reuben disqualified himself from leadership in the family, just as Simeon and Levi disqualified themselves at Shechem (Gen 49:5-7). The family leadership will fall to the fourth-born son, Judah (Gen 49:8-12).

> **Quick Bit:** The contents of Genesis 35 appear to be disjointed events and lists, but the narrator is pulling together many events from Jacob's life to summarize and also to prepare us for the story of Joseph. Notice how the chapter depends on all the stories leading up to it. Also think about how it sets the stage for the Joseph story.

After the incident between Reuben and Bilhah, the narrator provides a list of Jacob's 12 sons, listed according to their mothers: Leah had six sons (Reuben, Simeon, Levi, Judah, Issachar, and Zebulun); Rachel bore two sons (Joseph and Benjamin); Rachel's servant, Bilhah, had two sons (Dan and Naphtali); Leah's servant, Zilpah, had two sons (Gad and Asher). The classification of the sons according to their mothers reminds us of the competition and animosity between Rachel and Leah (Gen 29:31–30:24), preparing us for the family tensions that drive the story of Joseph (Gen 37–50).

In Genesis 35:27, Jacob finally reached his father's house at Mamre, where both Isaac and Abraham had lived. Rebekah's absence from the account suggests that she had died before Jacob arrived, never having seen her favorite son after he left home for Haran. When Isaac died, Esau and Jacob came together to bury him (Gen 35:29)—showing that their animosity has passed. In this moment of tragedy, there is some peace.

Jacob's life had come full circle. He had finally returned to his father's home, though now as a changed man. Despite the many pitfalls and wrong turns in Jacob's faith journey, God had remained faithful to this flawed patriarch, showering him with blessings, protecting him, and extending to him the covenant promises originally made to Abraham, despite his shortcomings. As Jacob observed God's longstanding faithfulness, he finally accepted the God of his forefathers as his own God. Jacob finally becomes Israel instead of Jacob, and thus becomes the namesake for the OT people of God.

As we continue to read Jacob's story, we will find that God's presence remains with Jacob, encouraging and protecting him throughout his life—even as he moves to Egypt during a severe famine (Gen 46:2–4). We will also see that Jacob remains committed to the God he has now embraced, passing on what he has learned about God's faithfulness to his favorite son, Joseph (Gen 48:21).

## THROUGHOUT THE BIBLE

Jacob first received his new name—Israel—from an unnamed man with whom he wrestled at Peniel (Gen 32:27–28). As Jacob returned to Bethel, the location of his first divine vision (Gen 28:10–22), God himself spoke to Jacob regarding his new name: "And God said to him, 'Your name is Jacob. Your name shall no longer be called Jacob, but Israel shall be your name'" (Gen 35:10). The name Israel (*yisra'el*), which likely means "God fights," signals not only a change in name, but a change in the direction of Jacob's life. Through this name change, Jacob, the patriarch who robbed his own brother of his birthright, became Israel, the eponymous head of a nation and kings (Gen 35:11).

Although the two names, Jacob and Israel, are used interchangeably throughout the biblical texts, the name "Israel" usually refers to the descendants of Jacob (compare Num 23:7). Yet the name is also used to refer to various other groups throughout the OT. It can denote all of God's people as the "children of Israel," the whole nation during the early monarchy, the northern kingdom during the period of the monarchy after Solomon, both the northern and southern kingdoms (e.g., Isa 8:14), and the land itself. For Jews, the name Israel came to carry connotations of the covenant, the theocratic nation of Israel, and the land given to God's people.

The name Israel is also used in similar ways in the NT. In the Gospels, for example, an angel of the Lord instructs Joseph to return the infant Jesus from Egypt to "the land of Israel" (Matt 2:20). When Jesus sent out the 12 disciples, whose number represents the tribes of Israel, he instructed them to avoid the Gentiles and Samaritans and instead to go only to "the lost sheep of the house of Israel." In Romans 9–11, Paul debates the identity of true Israel and its fate. And in the book of Revelation, the new Jerusalem is described as bearing the names of the 12 tribes of the sons of Israel (Rev 21:12).

All these uses of the name Israel in the OT and NT are rooted in the narrative of Jacob in Genesis, where God called him from a past of deception to a future as the head of God's people.

## BEYOND THE BIBLE

Jacob's journey of faith took a long and winding path. His return to Bethel after his initial encounter with God more than 20 years earlier finally signals a genuine acceptance of his role in God's plan. But ancient authors were not content that Jacob's turn toward righteousness occurred so late in life. Building on the depiction of Jacob in Genesis 25:27, they expanded the stories from later in Jacob's life to attribute a lifelong righteous perfection to him.

Genesis 25:27 says Israel was a "peaceful man." The Hebrew word for "peaceful," *tam*, is variously translated as "quiet," "peaceful," or "plain" in Genesis 25:27. The problem is that *tam* doesn't literally mean "quiet" or "peaceful"; it literally means "perfect," "whole," or "complete." Idiomatically, the term refers to everything from physical wholeness (i.e., health) to social conformity (i.e., well-mannered) to ethical uprightness. Here the original nuance is probably indicating Israel was well-mannered compared to Esau, but early interpreters latched on to the word's possible connotation of ethical perfection. The book of *Jubilees* narrates two conversations where Rebekah describes Israel after his return to Canaan.

> And [Rebekah] said [to Jacob], "My son, all my days I have never seen against you anything perverse but only uprightness." ... [Later, Rebekah said to Isaac, "Esau] is bitter against you because you blessed Jacob, your perfect and upright son, because he has no evil but only goodness" (*Jub.* 35:6, 12).[7]

In both cases, Rebekah's vision of Jacob is one of total moral perfection. Earlier in her conversation with Isaac, she describes Esau as the personification of evil, while Jacob is the exact opposite.

The tendency to rewrite Jacob as a righteous character existed in both Jewish and Christian traditions.[8] Ultimately, the goal was to justify that Jacob was worthy of receiving the blessing and birthright. Yet one of the recurring themes of the Bible is that God blesses people beyond what they deserve; he shows mercy to the undeserving. God's choice of Jacob despite his imperfections shows there's hope for all of us to find God despite our faults.

## APPLICATION

Jacob struggled throughout his life to commit himself fully to God. It isn't until the last chapter of the Jacob narrative (Gen 24–35) that he finally embraced the God of his forefathers as his God. When he did this, he put away the idols in his household. Then he and the members of his household purified themselves and put on new garments.

The act of putting away idols and changing garments illustrates what it means to repent. When Paul preached to the crowds at Lystra, he pleaded with the people to turn from their idols to the living God (Acts 14:15). He later exhorts the Ephesian Christians to "put off" their old habits and "put on" a new lifestyle that suits a new creation (Eph 4:23–24). Following God means turning away from a former way of living and embracing God's way of living. It means embracing the God of Abraham, Isaac, and Jacob as the only God. It means embracing Christ, and a relationship with him, as the way and means to do so (John 3:16–17).

Some of us are like Jacob in our faltering journeys of faith. Our commitment to God seems to come and go as we wrestle with fears or struggle for control. But the flawed Jacob kept his vow to Yahweh, and he stands as a testimony to God's patient work in people. The comfort of Jacob's story is that God remained faithful no matter what Jacob did. God's covenant with Abraham and his descendants survived Jacob's shortcomings because God is sovereign and gracious. God doesn't give up on people or his plans.

# DISCUSSION

**A Closer Look**

1. Have you ever felt like God "showed up" for other people, but not for you? Has there been a time when you realized he also "showed up" for you?

_____

_____

_____

2. Why did God allow (or choose) for his blessings to come through Israel? How is this encouraging for you?

_____

_____

_____

**Throughout the Bible**

1. God's gift of the name Israel was a great privilege for the patriarch. What privileges and responsibilities has God given to you?

_____

_____

_____

2. Think of something that you left behind—a facet of your life that was completely changed—when you became a believer. How did your new identity in Christ help you move forward?

_____

_____

_____

**Beyond the Bible**

1. Describe your own faith journey. What ups and downs have you experienced?

_____

_____

_____

2. Reflect on who you look up to as a spiritual mentor or leader. What qualities do they have that stand out as most helpful for your spiritual growth?

_____

_____

_____

**Application**

1. What keeps you from wholeheartedly following God through a relationship with Christ? What might you gain or lose if you fully commit to him?

_____

_____

_____

2. What old habits do you need to "put off" repeatedly? What new habits can take their place?

_____

_____

_____

# CONCLUSION

Until late in his life, Jacob's story goes completely as expected, just like God had spoken. He strives with his brother in the womb and continues to strive with others throughout his life. In the process, he becomes a servant when he should be an heir, albeit an heir of an inheritance and promise he had stolen. When he eventually bows down to his rival brother, he reaches a place of restoration and faith that his old self would probably never have achieved. Jacob shows himself to be redeemable: God gets ahold of him, and Jacob consequently recognizes that his bargaining and wrestling with God must stop. He must allow God to work through him. Jacob also recognizes that God truly has been with him all along, even in his darkest hours. This does not prevent Jacob from making more mistakes, but it certainly shows God's power to change a heart—and his faithfulness even when people are unfaithful.

We often look to the patriarchs for examples of great faith or virtue, but Jacob shows us more negative examples than positive ones. His story, narrated in vivid detail, testifies to the greatness of God. There is hope for all people—no one is too far removed or too stubborn for God to reach them and change their life.

The lesson of Jacob's life—one he only learns near the end when God changes his name to Israel—is that God fights for us. God is not against us, and he is not one to be bargained with, as Jacob thought. God cannot be manipulated like those whose heels Jacob grabbed in his struggle to get ahead. God fights alongside us, and he is the leader. We must set aside what we think is the best way to move forward and seek the one who will fight for us in each situation. We must put on a new self, like Jacob put on his new name, Israel, and embrace all that God has called us to be.

As we seek to discern God's presence in our lives, we must realize that he is there always, in every situation. We must look to the great calling he has given us and live it fully.

Jacob's relationship with God was uncertain and even conditional. But because of Jesus' death and resurrection, we can have a sure relationship with God in Christ through the Holy Spirit. Christ's sacrifice provides forgiveness of every sin we have committed, and the presence of his Spirit gives us continual access to the throne of God himself. We can decide that today is the day we will begin to live in relationship with Jesus, every moment until the end of our lives. We can turn from deception, lies, manipulation—the constant striving and wrestling—and embrace the God who made his presence known in the world so that he could change our lives (John 15–17). We can make the decision to mark today as the turning point.

# NOTES

## Chapter 1

1.  For more details on the life of Abraham, see Michael R. Grigoni, et al., *Abraham: Following God's Promise* (Studies in Faithful Living; Bellingham, Wash.: Logos Bible Software, 2012).
2.  Victor P. Hamilton, "Marriage: Old Testament and Ancient Near East," ed. David Noel Freedman et al., *The Anchor Yale Bible Dictionary*, Volume 4 (New York: Doubleday, 1992), 564.
3.  James B. Pritchard, ed., "Code of Hammurabi, lines 159-61," in *Ancient Near Eastern Texts Relating to the Old Testament*, 3rd ed. with Supplement (Princeton: Princeton University Press, 1969), 173.
4.  On the phenomenon of "oracular ambiguity," see T. A. Perry, "Cain's Sin in Gen. 4:1-7: Oracular Ambiguity and How to Avoid It," *Prooftexts: A Journal of Jewish Literary History* 25 (2005): 258-75. Other examples of this type of vague divine pronouncement in Genesis include Genesis 4:7, 15:1, and 16:11-12.
5.  James H. Charlesworth, *The Old Testament Pseudepigrapha*, vol. 2 (New York: Doubleday, 1985), 54.
6.  Ibid., 92.

## Chapter 2

1.  Victor P. Hamilton, *The Book of Genesis, Chapters 18-50*, The New International Commentary on the Old Testament (Grand Rapids, Mich.: Eerdmans, 1995), 183.
2.  Gordon J. Wenham, *Genesis 16-50*, Word Biblical Commentary, vol. 2. (Dallas: Thomas Nelson, 1998), 205.
3.  Ibid., 208.
4.  Bruce K. Waltke and Cathi J. Fredricks, *Genesis: A Commentary* (Grand Rapids, Mich.: Zondervan, 2001), 380-81.
5.  Walter Brueggemann, *Genesis*, Interpretation (Atlanta, Ga.: John Knox Press, 1982), 220.
6.  From *Midrash Leqaḥ Tob* 27:19 cited from James L. Kugel, *The Bible As It Was* (Cambridge, Mass.: Harvard University Press, 1997), 209.
7.  Ibid.

## Chapter 3

1. Brueggemann, 243.
2. Philo, *De Somniis* 1:150–6. Philo of Alexandria, *The Works of Philo: Complete and Unabridged*, trans. C. D. Yonge (Peabody, Mass.: Hendrickson, 1995), 378–9.
3. *Homilies on Genesis* 54.18 cited from Mark Sheridan, *Genesis 12–50*, Ancient Christian Commentary on Scripture, Old Testament 2 (Downers Grove, Ill.: InterVarsity Press, 2002), 191.

## Chapter 4

1. Abraham's servant is not identified by name, but he is possibly the Eliezer mentioned in Genesis 15:2.
2. D. P. O'Mathuna, "Divination, Magic," in *Dictionary of the Old Testament: Pentateuch,* edited by T. Desmond Alexander and David W. Baker (Downers Grove, Ill.: InterVarsity Press, 2003), 195.
3. Ephrem the Syrian, *Commentary on Genesis* 28.1.1 cited from Sheridan, *Genesis 12–50,* 199.
4. John Chrysostom, Homilies on Genesis 56.14 cited from Sheridan, *Genesis 12–50,* 198.

## Chapter 5

1. Sarna, 212.
2. Wenham, 256. See also Sarna, 212.
3. Sarna, 212.
4. Wenham, 256. See also J. J. Finkelstein, "An Old Babylonian Herding Contract and Genesis 31:38f," *Journal of the American Oriental Society* 88, no. 1 (1968): 30–36.
5. *Targum Onqelos* Genesis 31:19. See Kugel, *Bible As It Was,* 223.
6. Josephus, *The Antiquities of the Jews* 1.310–1 cited from Flavius Josephus, *The Works of Josephus: Complete and Unabridged,* trans. William Whiston (Peabody, Mass.: Hendrickson, 1987).
7. *Genesis Rabba* 74:5. See Kugel, *Bible As It Was,* 224.

## Chapter 6

1. From the Greek words *theos* ("god") and *phaino* ("to appear").
2. Waltke and Fredricks, 437.
3. Sarna, 231.
4. Origen, "De Principiis," trans. Frederick Crombie, in *The Ante-Nicene Fathers,* Volume IV (ed. Alexander Roberts et al.; Buffalo, N.Y.: The Christian Literature Company, 1885), 333.

## Chapter 7

1. Or by what we might call statutory rape, that is, the girl was too young to give consent. In the ancient Near East, unmarried women never had the right of consent.

2. John H. Walton, *Zondervan Illustrated Bible Backgrounds Commentary (Old Testament) Volume 1: Genesis, Exodus, Leviticus, Numbers, Deuteronomy* (Grand Rapids, Mich.: Zondervan, 2009), 118.

3. John H. Walton, Victor H. Matthews, and Mark W. Chavalas, *The IVP Bible Background Commentary: Old Testament* (Downers Grove, Ill.: InterVarsity Press, 2000), Genesis 34:2–12.

4. Walton, *Zondervan Illustrated*, 118.

5. Sarna, 233.

6. Ibid, 233–34.

## Chapter 8

1. Jacob's vow to give a tithe would most likely have been carried out through sacrifice since there was no established priesthood.

2. Sarna, 216.

3. James B. Pritchard, ed., "Mesopotamian Legal Documents: Nuzi Akkadian," in *Ancient Near Eastern Texts Relating to the Old Testament*, 3rd ed. with Supplement (Princeton: Princeton University Press, 1969), 219–20.

4. Hamilton, *The Book of Genesis, Chapters 18–50*, 377–78.

5. Sarna, 241.

6. Ibid., 244.

7. Charlesworth, 122–23.

8. Kugel, *Bible As It Was*, 200–201.

# SOURCES

Alexander, T. Desmond, and David W. Baker, eds. *Dictionary of the Old Testament: Pentateuch*. Downers Grove, Ill.: InterVarsity Press, 2003.

Barry, John D., and Lazarus Wentz, eds. *The Lexham Bible Dictionary*. Bellingham, Wash.: Logos Bible Software, 2012.

Bromiley, Geoffrey W., ed. *The International Standard Bible Encyclopedia, Revised*. 4 vols. Grand Rapids, Mich.: Eerdmans, 1988.

Brueggemann, Walter. *Genesis*. Interpretation. Atlanta, Ga.: John Knox, 1982.

Charlesworth, James H., ed. *The Old Testament Pseudepigrapha*. Vol. 2. New York: Doubleday, 1985.

Elwell, Walter A., ed. *Evangelical Dictionary of Biblical Theology*. Electronic ed. Grand Rapids, Mich.: Baker Book House, 1997.

Finkelstein, J. J. "An Old Babylonian Herding Contract and Genesis 31:38f." *Journal of the American Oriental Society* 88, No. 1 (1968): 30–36.

Freedman, David Noel, et al., eds. *The Anchor Yale Bible Dictionary*. New York: Doubleday, 1992.

Grigoni, Michael R., Miles Custis, Douglas Mangum, and Matthew M. Whitehead. *Abraham: Following God's Promise*. Bellingham, Wash.: Logos Bible Software, 2012.

Hamilton, Victor P. *The Book of Genesis, Chapters 18–50*. The New International Commentary on the Old Testament. Grand Rapids, Mich.: Eerdmans, 1995.

Josephus, Flavius. *The Works of Josephus: Complete and Unabridged*. Translated by William Whiston. Peabody, Mass.: Hendrickson, 1987.

Kugel, James L. *The Bible as It Was*. Cambridge, Mass.: Belknap Press of Harvard University Press, 1997.

Mathews, K. A. *Genesis 11:27–50:26*. Vol. 1B. The New American Commentary. Nashville: Broadman & Holman, 2005.

McKeown, James. *Genesis*. The Two Horizons Old Testament Commentary. Grand Rapids, Mich.: Eerdmans, 2008.

Perry, T. A. "Cain's Sin in Gen. 4:1–7: Oracular Ambiguity and How to Avoid It." *Prooftexts: A Journal of Jewish Literary History* 25 (2005): 258–75.

Philo of Alexandria. *The Works of Philo: Complete and Unabridged*. Translated by C. D. Yonge. Peabody, Mass.: Hendrickson, 1995.

Pritchard, James B., ed. *Ancient Near Eastern Texts Relating to the Old Testament*. 3rd ed. with Supplement. Princeton: Princeton University Press, 1969.

Roberts, Alexander, James Donaldson, and A. Cleveland Coxe, eds. *The Ante-Nicene Fathers*. Vol. IV. Buffalo, N. Y.: The Christian Literature Company, 1885.

Ryken, Leland, James C. Wilhoit, and Tremper Longman III, eds. *Dictionary of Biblical Imagery*. Electronic ed. Downers Grove, Ill.: InterVarsity Press, 2000.

Sailhamer, John H. "Genesis." In *The Expositor's Bible Commentary, Volume 2: Genesis, Exodus, Leviticus, Numbers*, edited by Frank E. Gaebelein, 1–284. Grand Rapids, Mich.: Zondervan, 1990.

Sarna, Nahum M. *Genesis*. The JPS Torah Commentary. Philadelphia: The Jewish Publication Society, 1989.

Sheridan, Mark. *Genesis 12–50*. Vol. Old Testament II. Ancient Christian Commentary on Scripture. Downers Grove, Ill.: InterVarsity Press, 2002.

Tenney, Merrill C., and Moisés Silva, eds. *The Zondervan Encyclopedia of the Bible*. 5 vols. Revised, Full-Color Edition. Grand Rapids, Mich.: Zondervan, 2009.

Waltke, Bruce K., and Cathi J. Fredricks. *Genesis: A Commentary*. Grand Rapids, Mich.: Zondervan, 2001.

Walton, John H. *Genesis*. The NIV Application Commentary. Grand Rapids, Mich.: Zondervan, 2001.

Walton, John H., Victor Harold Matthews, and Mark W. Chavalas. *The IVP Bible Background Commentary: Old Testament*. Downers Grove, Ill.: InterVarsity Press, 2000.

Wenham, Gordon J. *Genesis 16–50*. Word Biblical Commentary, Vol. 2. Dallas, Tex.: Word, 1998.

# ABOUT THE EDITOR

**John D. Barry** is the publisher of Lexham Press, general editor of Faithlife Study Bible and *Lexham Bible Dictionary*, and the previous editor-in-chief of *Bible Study Magazine*. He is the author of *The Resurrected Servant in Isaiah* and over 100 articles, as well as the coauthor of *Connect the Testaments: A Daily Devotional with Bible Reading Plan* and *Mary: Discerning God's Presence*.

# ABOUT THE AUTHORS

**Derek R. Brown** is a contributing editor for the Lexham Bible Guides: Paul's Letters Collection. He holds a PhD in New Testament Studies and Christian Origins from the University of Edinburgh and a Master of Arts in New Testament Studies from Regent College.

**Miles Custis** is the author of *The End of the Matter: Understanding the Epilogue of Ecclesiastes*, a Faithlife Study Bible contributing editor, the coauthor of Lexham Bible Guides: Genesis Collection, and the coauthor of *Jacob: Discerning God's Presence* and three other Studies in Faithful Living volumes. In addition, he is a regular *Bible Study Magazine* and *Lexham Bible Dictionary* contributor. He holds a Master of Arts in biblical studies from Trinity Western University.

**Douglas Mangum** is the editor of the Lexham Bible Guides series and the Lexham Methods Series, the coauthor of Lexham Bible Guides: Genesis Collection, and the coauthor of *Mary: Discerning God's Presence* and three other Studies in Faithful Living volumes. He is a Lexham English Bible editor, a Faithlife Study Bible contributing editor, a regular *Bible Study Magazine* contributor, and a frequently consulted specialist for the *Lexham Bible Dictionary*. In addition, he is a PhD candidate in Near Eastern studies at the University of Free State; he holds a Master of Arts in Hebrew and Semitic studies from the University of Wisconsin–Madison.

**Wendy Widder** holds a PhD in Near Eastern studies from the University of the Free State, an MA in Hebrew and Semitic Studies from the University of Wisconsin–Madison, and an MDiv from Grand Rapids Theological Seminary. She is the author of *Living Whole Without a Better Half*, *A Match Made in Heaven: How Singles and the Church Can Live Happily After*, and the coauthor of *The Forest and the Trees: Helping Teachers Integrate a Biblical Worldview Across the Curriculum*.

# JACOB
### DISCERNING GOD'S PRESENCE

Keep studying Jacob with your entire church: pick up the complete digital curriculum

## Personal workbook

Biblical, cultural, and historical
background, plus applications
and reflection questions

## Leader's guide

The key to the complete curriculum,
with sermon outlines and downloads
for media and handouts

## Presentation slides

Both sermon and small group
versions available in PowerPoint and
Keynote, standard and high definition

## Sermon outlines

Weekly lesson outlines and
discussion questions, with
space for notes and reflections

## Group handouts

Key passages, learning objectives,
and prompts for slides and videos,
available in Word and PDF

## Videos

Introductory videos for each
week's session—plus a bumper
video to promote the series

*Jacob: Discerning God's Presence Church Curriculum* helps your entire church
dig deeper into the life of Jacob. Plus, our digital resources sync across
platforms, so you can take your study with you anytime, anywhere.

# Equip your church today!

LexhamPress.com/SFL-Jacob　◦　1-800-875-6467 (US)　◦　+1 360-527-1700 (Int'l)

LEXHAM PRESS

LOGOS
Bible Software

# Discover More with Lexham Press

Each volume in the Not Your Average Bible Study series guides you step-by-step through Scripture, helping you discover powerful insights as you move through the text, digging into the Bible on a whole new level. With discussion and reflection questions, specific prayer suggestions, and ideas for further study, you'll see how easy it is to apply these lessons to your everyday life.

Much of what we learn serves an immediate purpose, but God's Word has eternal value. That's why it is vital that we seek His Spirit daily through prayer and Bible study. Connect the Testaments is a 365-day devotional with a custom reading plan that covers the entire Bible over one year, explaining difficult and complex passages along the way.

This rich collection of thoughtful sermons from one of the leading contemporary theologians is challenging, stimulating, and inspiring. These reflections, born from years of theological and biblical study, demonstrate the complexity of the realities we face in the Christian life and the depth of the grace of God.

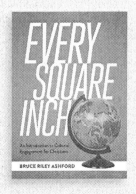

Drawing on such sources as Abraham Kuyper, Francis Schaeffer, and C.S. Lewis, Bruce Ashford argues that God wants our whole lives to be shaped by Jesus' lordship. If Jesus truly is Lord over everything, then our faith is relevant to every dimension of culture.